Thank You

I would like to thank my father, Maurice Frank, and my mother, Mildred Frank, for the direction that they have given me in my life. Without the valuable life lessons that they left me with, I would have never been able to write this book.

I would also like to thank my wife Ruthie, my sons, Michael and Brian, and my daughter, Jillian, for putting up with my ranting regarding the importance of changing the world that we live in.

I would also like to thank my brothers, Marv, Bob, Bill and Brad and Ruthies family, for their continuous support.

Thanks to the "One Voice Now" group and all the other wonderful friends who were always supportive and who never lost sight of the "vision."

And most of all, thank you to God for giving us this miraculous and necessary Communication Technology to empower us all and allow us to change for the better, the world that we live in.

Foreward

This book is dedicated to all of the people in America and around the world, in the past and the present, who have actively tried to make this world a better place for mankind.

With the 21st Century Communication Technology that is now available, along with the plan outlined in this book, nonviolent activists in the future will no longer have to endure the frustration, pain and even death that activists in the past have had to experience.

Ideas for making the world a better place for mankind, can now, simply flow.

David A. Frank

A special thanks to <u>Harry P. Singleton</u> for his belief in this cause and convincing me to write this book.

A special thanks to <u>Jennifer Taylor,</u> <u>Ann Korb</u> and <u>Aunt Rene Frank</u> for their kind assistance in editing this book.

Thanks to Nathan Sisler for his wonderful artwork.

ONE SINGLE MIND...

made up of 300 million people, each containing billions of brain cells...all working together to solve the problems of today... making the world a better place for the children of tomorrow.

THE PATH FROM A PATHETIC TO A PROPHETIC AMERICA...

PIECE BY PEACE

PROPHET: *One who speaks for God or a god, or as though, under a Divine Guidance. A spokesman for some cause, group, etc. One who predicts the future.*

PROPHETIC: *Having the powers of a Prophet.*

WE ALL HAVE THE ABILITY TO ENVISION THE "FUTURE."

We are all vessels. Just as a vessel at sea carries people and cargo, humans are vessels that carry ideas.

If you believe that we all came from a "Creator," you should not have a problem believing that we were all meant to be "creative." Being creative means that we have the ability to predict the future. We have the ability to envision an idea in our mind and, in the future, re-create that idea into a reality.

As my wife begins to sew a dress, in her mind she already knows what the future will bring. The future will bring a finished product of the idea that she sees in her mind.

We, as humans, all have the same ability. Although the pictures that we see in our minds may be different, each and everyone of us is capable of turning that idea in our minds into a reality for the future.

From an ordinary person like Famous Amos, turning his special cookie recipe into a product that the whole world can enjoy, to an ordinary person like Thomas Edison, taking his idea and lighting up the future and literally changing the world as we know it. From an ordinary person like Henry Ford imagining a world where people transport themselves in "horseless carriages," to an ordinary person like Adolf Hitler showing us how our world can be transformed into hell.

We all have the ability to envision an idea, and with our ideas, change the world that we live in. The ability to share our ideas with others is the trick. The ability for others to pick and choose the ideas that they need to make their own lives better is the goal.

The empowerment of the people and their ideas is what is missing in America and the world today. The ability to empower the people and their ideas is the answer.

Everything that humans have done on this planet is a result from a vision- from sticks to spears, from rocks to bullets, from caves to houses, from walking to standing on the Moon. Those ideas and visions are not a result of people in Washington D.C., State Capitals or political people downtown.

The ideas that have had the most profound effect on America came from "you the people," ordinary people with extraordinary ideas

The visions that are going to change America and the world now are not going to come from the people at the top of the hierarchy. They are going to come from "you the people."

In the present condition of America and countries around the world, we need the ideas and visions of "you the people" now more than ever before.

This book is going to lay out the plan for the year 2010. This plan will allow us to tap into those ideas and visions. It will talk about why our present system is not working, why it can`t work and how to peacefully transform it.

If America fails to plan, it will plan to fail. This is the plan that America now needs to change its direction and make this world a better place for its inhabitants. We now need a 21st Century system to deal with 21st Century problems.

TO UNDERSTAND WHERE WE ARE AND WHERE WE WANT TO GO, WE MUST FIRST UNDERSTAND WHERE WE HAVE BEEN...

AMERICA, PAST AND PRESENT

"Vote for me and I'll set you free." For the last fifty years, I have been listening to rhetoric like that and all I can say is that the people who were voted into office, whether it be on a Federal, State or local level, have done their best to turn a once wonderful, country into a pathetic place to live. Is "pathetic" a fair word to describe the greatest country on earth? If you could have seen the America that I grew up in, you too would use that term.

I remember growing up in a world where you could take off on your bike in the morning and return after dark without your parents having to worry about your well being.

Today, parents cannot take their eyes off of their children for more than a minute without worrying about someone snatching them up.

I remember walking to school and returning home for lunch that my mother had prepared.

Today, kids ride to school on a school bus all the way across town and return home sometimes hours after school is over.

I remember the doctor coming to my house when one of us was sick. We were able to pay him for the visit right out of our pocket because the amount that he charged was affordable.

Today, America's healthcare has become unaffordable or unavailable to tens of millions of American people and the number is growing every day. People are not only getting sick but are literally dying from lack of healthcare.

I remember having to take my bike to the fire station every year to register it. For 25 cents they gave you a little license plate. It was important. If you ever lost or had your bike stolen, they had records to match you up with the serial number on your bike if they ever found it.

Today it is no longer about registering something and paying a tax to benefit "you." It is about taxes imposed on just about every conceivable thing in your life to benefit the Federal, State or Local government. And, God help you if you don't or can't pay that tax on time. They will punish you like a red headed step child, with even more tax.

I remember watching programs on television where the stars of the show, slept in separate beds. "Damn" was the closest thing to a four-letter word that you would hear, and that was not on television but during the movie "Gone With the Wind."

Today's television programming allows us to watch people engaging in sex, and the use of profanity and portrayal of inconceivable violence is nothing out of the ordinary. Today's programming has allowed what is shown on televison to spill over into real life.

Parents could go to their kid's football games, basketball games, track meets, plays, recitals, fun fairs and other functions that the school had because the school was right down the street.

Today by the time parents get home from work, they do not have the time or energy to go all the way across town to participate like they used to.

Years ago neighborhoods were built around schools. Neighborhoods had sidewalks where people could walk or ride their bikes.

Today, it is difficult to build a neighborhood around a school when the school that your kid attends is all the way across town.

I remember going to locally owned businesses such as the grocery, the restaurants, the hardware store, the pharmacy, the clothing and the shoe store. Just about anything that you could think of or needed was owned by local people. When you needed something, the owner was there and he knew you by name. He asked how others in your family were doing and he really did care about the answer that you gave because he knew them all personally. He not only gave you personalized service but he answered your questions, provided advice and gave you information on the product that you were buying.

Today if you need something, you are on your own. Giant stores have come into the community and not only undercut locally owned businesses which are now only a memory. If you want to find something or need advice, you are pointed to an aisle by someone that is only working there because they desperately need a job.

Growing up in the early 50's wasn't all peaches and cream though. To tell you the truth, it was downright scary at times. They kept telling us about a situation called the "Cold War." Those people in Russia were crazy. At any moment, as crazy as those Russian people were, someone over there could have pushed a button and blown up America and the rest of the planet. We used to hide under our desks at school, preparing for the big moment. I really believed that hiding under that desk would have really helped to save me.

As time went on, we began to realize that not only were we afraid of those crazy Russians, but they were equally afraid of us Americans. As more time went by, we began to realize that it wasn't those Russian people that were so bad. It was their

11

Russian leaders that were crazy. As more time went by, we began to realize that it wasn't the American people that the Russian leaders were upset with; it was the American leaders. Whatever the American leaders did to the Russian leaders and vice versa, the citizens in both countries were caught in between. As more time went by, the "Cold War" began to cool off. The Russian people and the American people even became friends. It seemed, for a while, the leaders of both countries got somewhat civil to each other.

Sadly today, things have gotten even 'colder," for not only the citizens of America and Russia, but now children around the world have to grow up with the same fear that we had growing up. Unfortunately today, it is even worse. It is not just the crazy leaders in America and Russia threatening to destroy all human life on the planet; it is a multitude of crazy leaders wanting to get their hands on "the bomb."

In the winter time, I remember that the park department used to flood the tennis courts so that we could ice skate all winter long. We sat around bon fires and warmed ourselves until we were thawed enough to go back and skate some more.

Today if they did that, there would be a lawyer around every corner waiting to sue the city every time someone fell down.

I remember when the lawyers in this country thought that it

would be considered "unproffesional" to advertise.

Today, every other commercial is a law firm letting you know that they are willing to sue anybody for anything.

Not that long ago, America was the number "1" manufacturer in the world. We not only manufactured goods, we sold them and we serviced them. America was the place that people from around the world came to restart their lives. They knew it was the land of opportunity for anyone to make their vision a reality.

THEN CAME THE 90`s

And then, in the early 90`s, America started to change. Things not only went downhill, but became "pathetic" very quickly.

CEO`s of some of Americas companies, some of the finest and most profitable companies in the world, were strapping on their golden parachutes, filling their pockets with more money than they could spend in many lifetimes and guiding the American workers to their demise. The jobs that Americans once performed ended up being done by people in other countries. The jobs that once provided a fair wage are now being done by people that could be categorized as "slaves." The jobs that once provided the American people with an income and a future was becoming not only hard to find, but impossible.

Today, in the year 2010, America`s economy is now in the worst condition that I have seen it in my 62 years on this planet. Tens of millions of American people now live at or below the poverty level. This situation in other countries landed them the term "third world countries." Recent statistics tell us that, a very small, 5% of the population now owns over 80% of America's wealth. The rest of America, 95% of the population, now finds itself fighting each other over the 20% of the wealth that is left.

There are now over two and a half million people in jails and prisons. That number does not include the people going in everyday and those coming out. That number also does not include the people who are dramatically affected by having their loved ones in prison. Prisons in America have become an industry unto itself.

WE DID WHAT THEY ASKED US TO DO..

We voted for them, just like they had asked us to do. We had a Democrat President, with a Republican Congress. We had a Republican President with a Democrat Congress. We had a Democrat President with a Democrat Congress. We had a Republican President, with a Republican Congress. We even had the Independents sprinkled in all of the above.

Forever the Democrats have been telling the American people that the Republicans are incapable of solving America's problems. Forever the Republicans have been telling us that the Democrats are incapable of solving America's problems. In fact, they are accusing each other of being the culprit for America's problems. A large percentage of the American population is now awakening to the fact that both parties have, finally, been telling us the "truth."

Solving America's problems is not going to happen by replacing Democrats with Republicans or Republicans with Democrats. We have tried that for many years and America is now in worst shape than it has ever been. Even if they held hands and worked together, it is not going to make any difference. If they ever figured out that holding hands could make a difference, the only thing that they would figure out is that they could steal from the Americans faster and more efficiently.

In the year 2010, the Tea Party believes that the answer to solving America's problems is putting their candidates in office. The Green Party, the Libertarian Party and others believe the same thing. The reality is whoever you have filling these 535 seats in Washington D.C., the 150 seats in state capitals or the 20 or so downtown is not going to make any difference at all.

The fact still remains, when out of 300 million people in America, you have only 535 people making decisions for everyone, you have a "brain dead" system. The same holds true for 150 people in state capitals making decisions for six million people and 20 or so downtown making decisions for 300,000 people.

No matter whom we voted for, in the early 90's the majority from each party pushed a new economic system for America that would soon bankrupt the greatest country on earth. America now finds itself over 13 trillion dollars in debt with our manufacturing sent to other workers around the world, with no possible way, under our present system and situation, to pay it back.

The name of their plan was N.A.F.T.A., the "North American Free Trade Agreement." The plan was simple. They were going to take the fairly paid manufacturing jobs here in America and give those jobs to slaves in other countries.

They pushed it by explaining to the American people that this plan is something that you may not be intelligent enough to understand but it will benefit all of us in the long run. They even had their expert economists touting its benefit. Legislators even gave tax incentives to corporations that participated. It did not work well for the American workers, but it worked like a charm for the corporations, the CEO`s and their bottom line. Having the benefit of slave labor  to produce their goods gave the CEO`s and other heads of the corporations the obscene incomes and benefits that they enjoy today.

JOBS IN AMERICA BEFORE THE 90`S

I graduated from high school in 1967. One thing that none of us had to worry about at that time was finding a job. We knew that we could find a job right out of high school or if we wanted to go to the next step with our education, college, there would be a job out there waiting for us.

Today, in the year 2010, the job market is "pathetic." Without jobs, the American dream cannot become a reality. Without jobs, the crime rate increases exponentially. We not only have more people in jails and prisons than ever before, we now have more people on antidepressants and other mood and mind altering drugs than ever before. We now have a divorce rate that is higher than ever before. We now have a bankruptcy rate that is higher than ever before. We now have a high school dropout rate that is higher than ever before. We now have a suicide rate that is of epidemic proportion and higher than ever before.

THE PURPOSE OF THIS BOOK IS TO "CHANGE THE SYSTEM."...WOULD THE INVENTORS OF OUR PRESENT, 225 YEAR OLD SYSTEM, GIVE US THEIR BLESSING?

Actually, our Founding Fathers implied in the Declaration of Independence that changing our present system was not forbidden, it was expected. The same people who devised the present system that we struggle to live with never expected it to survive this long. Although some would believe that it may be, somehow, sacrilegious or even blasphemous to consider a new and better working system of self-direction and self-empowerment, our Founding Fathers would call this action "courageous."

Thomas Jefferson, drafter of the Declaration of Independence and a political genius of the ages, stated that he believed there should be a revolution every 20 years because "the tree of liberty needed nourishing from the blood of tyrants." The duty to establish a new system of government need not be as drastic as suggested by Jefferson.

The Declaration of Independence, however, states these enduring facts:

1. "We hold these truths to be self-evident, that all men are created equal." In its purest sense, this statement means that all

people in America should have an equal "voice" in the destiny of our country.

2. "That they are endowed by their creator with certain inalienable rights." Inalienable means rights that are incapable of being surrendered or transferred and is understood to mean that these rights proceed from God. Never is it to be understood that inalienable rights come from a handful of public servants. If rights are to be changed in any way, that change should be decided by the people themselves.

3. "That among these are Life, Liberty and the pursuit of Happiness. That to secure these rights Governments are instituted among men, deriving their just powers from the consent of the governed." Deriving their "just powers" means that determining issues of the nation as well as the answers to these issues are to come from the people. We now realize that it is the people themselves that are left to live with the decisions that are made.

4. "That whenever any form of Government becomes destructive of these ends, it is the right of the people to alter or to abolish it, and to institute new Government, laying its foundation on such principles and organizing its powers in such form; as to them shall seem most likely to affect their safety and happiness." Who, other than the people themselves, having a direct voice, can determine what comprises their own safety and happiness?

5. "But when a long train of abuses and usurpations, pursuing invariably the same object evinces a design to reduce them under absolute despotism, [How many families must live on the streets to reach this level?], it is their right, it is their duty, to throw off such Government, and to provide new guards for their future security." (How high do taxes have to reach before we realize that it is our money, the object that was referred to, that has left so many in absolute despotism?)

The preceding five points quoted from the Declaration of Independence, in my estimation, were penned by our Founding Fathers as the blueprint of action to follow in case the Republic they had started may not have been able to stand the test of time. They therefore pronounced it is not only our right, but more courageously our duty to institute a new system as modern as the times would permit. In essence, our Founding Fathers are telling us across space and time that we must do whatever it takes to survive, just as they did over 200 years ago.

The concept behind the Declaration of Independence is about the most valuable thing that man can fight for. It gives us Freedom. People over 200 years ago had to fight for it. People of today have to fight for it. The question is: do we want to fight for it like they did and kill people in the process, or would we rather use our heads and our voices to save lives, rather than waste lives? There is no doubt in my mind. Killing sets the precedent for a society that kills. Living and allowing to let live sets the precedent for a society of Love and Life. This short book sets the direction for the latter.

I can go on and on talking about the societal problems that America is now facing but that is not the purpose of this book. The purpose of this book is to talk about a solution to these problems, to talk about a tool that we now have available to all of us so that we can role up our sleeves together and start solving these problems, problems that the people that we voted for were not able to solve. In fact, they are the reason that these problems have taken us to this pathetic level.

The name of their profession even implies that they are the ones responsible for America's present condition. "Politics" when dissected means "poli" or "many and "tics" or "blood suckers."

They, from the Federal, to the State, to the Local, have done an excellent job at sucking the blood out of America and its people.

The word "Congress" also does an excellent job at describing its role in America. We know that the word "progress" means to "move forward." "I will let you decide what the word "Con-gress" implies. Isn't it ironic that with the decisions that have been made for us by "Congress" that America is no longer moving in the "forward direction?"

I became an "activist" in 1990 for two reasons. The first reason was because of an experience that I had that changed my life. Let me tell you about the second reason, first.

The second reason was N.A.F.T.A. When I first heard about N.A.F.T.A., I went sort of crazy. First of all, I could not believe that the people in Washington D.C. could be not only that stupid, but that diabolical. How could anyone intentionally sabotage this country so openly, right out in front of everyone?

The majority of the politicians in Washington promoted this thing like it was going to be greater than sliced bread, like this was the answer that was going to take this great nation and make it even greater. I could not only figure out how the politicians could do this but even more so how could the American people accept this? How could everyone in America not be going absolutely crazy when this was presented to them? How could every politician that has ever put his name on legislation promoting this "economic hijacking of America" not be indicted for treason, for intentionally wrecking this great country?

N.A.F.T.A. was the second thing that got my attention. The first thing that got me off of my dead ass and turned me into an activist happened one week before Christmas, 1989. To this day, I can't explain it but also, to this day, I cannot deny it. The following is a description of my first life changing experience.

THE VISION

I have always believed that the United States of America is the most wonderful country on earth. To this day, no one can convince me of the contrary. I had always felt that special people were running America. I felt that those people had a higher knowledge than most ordinary citizens. My views have changed 180 degrees from my initial belief. I now believe that the people who make decisions for America, who decide what direction American and its people are going to take, have less knowledge than the average citizen.

There is no doubt that 300 million citizens hold millions of times more information and knowledge than the people in Washington, state capitals and local governments. In fact, the amount of intelligence in those 535 politicians in Washington compared to the amount of intelligence, collectively, in 300 million people is comparable to a grain of sand on the beach. It is the difference between a library containing 535 books of information compared to a library containing 300 million books of information.

The information that made me realize this was presented to me one week before Christmas, 1989. It was an occurrence that changed my life and totally changed my way of thinking. I realized that it was the common citizen that held the key to the future direction and success of America. It was information that made me realize that by changing our system, thus changing the way America thinks, other countries would soon follow.

One week before Christmas, 1989, at exactly 5:45 A.M., my eyes opened. I was in a state of paralysis. I could not get up. I could not go back to sleep. I was forced to lay there with my eyes opened. I was forced to watch a replay of my life being shown on my bedroom window blinds.

I have heard people who describe near-death experiences. They tell of how their life flashed before them in a matter of seconds. My life, too, was flashing before me. The difference is that it was not a matter of seconds. It was as though I was watching a movie being played at normal speed.

As I was growing up, I had always felt as though there were experiences in my life that I had no control over. I felt as though these were paths in my life that I had to travel for one reason or another. I now realized the importance of those journeys. There were several of those experiences that were picked out and replayed to me. They were basically negative experiences that were now beginning to make more sense than ever.

As I watched this review of my life, I was now able to watch them as almost an innocent bystander, a person who was able to recapture the emotional feelings from the experience but also a person able to stand back, years later, and understand the valuable lesson that came from the experience.

As each experience unfolded, I was able to recall the pain but also the reason that caused me to venture down that negative path in the first place. By combining those two senses, I began to realize that my own experiences were situations that not only myself, but millions of other people faced as well. I was starting to understand that the situations that I once found myself in were necessary to piece together information that was being given to me to explain how America worked. I was not only learning how America worked, I was being shown how it didn't work. I was released from my first "class" one hour and fifteen minutes later. It was 7:00 a.m. exactly. My wife was laying next to me, sleeping soundly and not budging an inch the entire time of my vision. When I was released, although the experience was scary and, at the same time, enlightening, I forced myself to "blow it off."

Although I couldn't get it off of my mind, I started rationalizing it by calling it a "mini stroke." Whatever it was, it did not seem natural. I went to work that morning. I owned a restaurant in the hometown of the Notre Dame "Fighting Irish," South Bend, Indiana. Our restaurant was called "Frank's Red Hots." It was a deli known for its Chicago Style hot dogs. My wife Ruthie and I started our dream restaurant six years earlier when we decided that people were hamburgered out. We thought that South Bend needed a great hot dog.

Although tired and confused, I entered my building trying to act as though nothing out of the ordinary had happened. I thought that I was doing a pretty good job until just about everyone kept asking if I felt all right. Trying not to make anyone aware of my experience, I defensively replied that I was fine. I must have looked pretty rough.

As the day passed and everyday problems started occurring, my memory of my early morning experience was fading. Every time that it popped into my mind, I blew it off as an unpleasant, freak moment that I was glad was over. Little did I know that I was far from right about that.

The next morning at exactly 5:45 A.M., here it came again. More reviews of more of my life. Experiences that I thought were long gone were being replayed as if they were yesterday. Experiences were methodically picked to drive home a point that needed to be made. From spending three days in jail in 1977 to my divorce, all of the key moments in my life were being replayed and being used to make me understand life itself, for me and millions of other people. On my second day of class, I became more belligerent. I tried to escape the grip of paralysis that was being forced upon me. I wanted no more of this class. The lessons of life were making me aware of some things that I did not want to know. I was beginning to feel as though this information was being given to me to get me to respond, to get me to do something that I never even dreamed of doing. I was beginning to feel as though I were being groomed to pass on some information that would do something of tremendous magnitude for America.

After all, doing things of magnitude is for the special people who run our country, or so I thought. Once again, at 7:00 A.M., I was released from my class. Once again, I refused to believe that this was really happening to me. I looked over at my wife and could not believe that she had just slept through my second encounter of a weird kind.

At work, my second day, nothing changed much from the first day. Once again, people were looking at me as though I was walking death. I got tired of the suggestion that maybe I should go home and get some sleep.

Along came the third, fourth and fifth day. Each day at 5:45 my day would begin, and at 7:00 I was released out into the real world. Each day, I began to feel as though I was being pumped with more and more pieces of the puzzle of life and no one else around me was able to see what was shown to me.

On the fifth day of my visions, we had gone to a friend's house for dinner. This was the first time that I realized how much trouble I was in. This was the first time that I realized that my life would never be the same.

After a great dinner, the guys went into the living room to shoot the bull. Usually on an occasion like this, sports or something of mundane interest is the topic of choice. Not true for me.

All of a sudden I found myself standing up and getting real serious. I found myself saying things like "Don't you understand what they are doing to us? They are taking are money and giving us these greedy hypocritical laws to live under." Needless to say, the party got real serious and nobody really wanted to hear what I had to say. I couldn't understand why they didn't feel the same way I felt. Things got unbelievably cold, and my wife escorted me quickly out to the car as though I just killed someone.

She could not believe that I could say things like that at a party that was supposed to be fun. "People just don't want to hear things like that," she would say. After that, the ride home was very quiet. I thought I had more trouble than I could handle. All of a sudden, here I am, understanding things about America that no one else seems to know and definitely doesn't want to talk about. Just as I thought my life could not get any worse, the sixth day proved me wrong.

I awoke at the usual time on the sixth day, but this time it was different. This time instead of a review of my life and the lessons to be learned from it, this time I was receiving information that would scare the hell out of me. I was being given the answer to the question that everyone who wants a beautiful future for themselves and their children was looking for.

There seemed to be an electric field around my head. I could not raise my arms because of my paralyzed state, but if I could have, I believe that my hair was standing-on- end. Not only was there an electrical field around my head, but this time it felt as though someone or something was being dropped into my body. It felt as though I was sharing my body with someone else, someone that I may have known, possibly in a past life. All of these feelings were surrounding me, as the answer was being given me to give to all.

The answer is in three parts. The first part is that the television is a miracle that has been given to us, by God, not to sell us sex and violence and overpriced tennis shoes. It has been given to us to allow "we, the people" to hear debates on issues that affect our lives and our future.

The second part is that the touch-tone phone has been given to us, by God, not to have phone sex with someone, but to allow us to vote directly on the issues ourselves, after we review debates over the television.

The third part is that the computer is a miracle given to us by God, not so that the IRS knows how much money you make before you do. It has been given to us so that when we vote, using any touch-tone phone, those calls can go into a computer downtown where we are each registered with I.D. numbers. When we vote on issues, the computer will receive the calls and by punching an ID number into your touch-tone phone, the computer will check your ID number, allow you to vote "yes" or "no" on an issue and block you out from being able to vote twice. By combining these three components, or miracles from God, we can now have decisions made of, by and for the people.

As this information was being given to me, I felt that emotionally I was being put through the wringer. Not only was I being controlled, but someone was now sharing my body, and at the same time information so valuable was being given to me that I had tears rolling down my cheeks. I have never been so scared in my life.

At 7:00, I was released once again, and once again, I looked over at my wife, and she lay there sound asleep as though nothing was going on. I was not going to go through this alone any longer. I hopped out of bed yelling, "Honey, wake up. That's it.

This is what we have been waiting for. The television has been given to us by God. It's been given to us so that we, the people, can hear the issues debated ourselves. The touch-tone phone is a miracle from God. It's been given to us so that we, the people, can call in and vote on the issues. The computer is a miracle from God. It's been given to us, not so the IRS can steal from us. It's been given to us so that the calls can go into the computer, and the computer can count the votes and make sure each person votes only one time. We can finally have decisions made by we, the people." She looked at me as if I was the craziest person on the planet. She looked as though she had just lost a good husband.

The seventh morning was just a review of the sixth. Once again, the electric field was around my head. Once again, it felt as though someone or something was being dropped into my body and once again the answer was being given to me.

After I was released at 7:00, I started explaining to my wife, after I woke her out of a sound sleep, that the three miracles that I spoke of were miracles from God and were given to us to help the people, not hurt the people. Once again came the same look from my wife that she had just lost a good husband.

I thank God that I am married to the person that I am. Even though the initial shock took us both by surprise, she has supported me and the message given to me 100%. She is without a doubt the person that I was meant to be with the only person that I can think of that could take a situation as strange as this and get behind it. How would you like to be married to someone who actually believes that he can change the world?

Most things that have occurred to me in my life have been out of my control. Meeting and falling in love with my wife was one of those situations. I thank God for that every day.

TODAY...

Today, the American people are being asked to vote on American Idol, Dancing With the Stars, Miss America, issues presented on CNN, Fox, CNBC, MSNBC and a multitude of other programs. The results of those votes sometimes make a difference but most of the time, go nowhere at all. We are presently voting, having our voices heard, on issues that will **not** really make a difference in our lives.

We can now, heading into the year 2011, put the necessary Communication Technology in place, in our own communities, that will allow " we the people" to start voting on issues in our community that can make all of the difference in the world as to what kind of world we are going to live in.

We are being asked today to vote on talent in America, beauty in America and other unimportant issues. With a new plan for America, we can now start having our voices heard on the most important issues in our lives.

We can have our voices heard on our community education system, our tax system, where we want our tax money to be spent, our environment, ideas for a new healthcare system in our community and numerous other ideas designed to make our communities, our piece of America, better for ourselves, our families and future generations.

Instead of voting for "politicians" to vote on issues that you are interested in; why not just use "21ˢᵗ Century Communication Technology" and just <u>vote on the issues yourself?</u>

In the year 2010 we are able to use the television for finding information that can better our lives. We now have access to channels such as the Travel Channel, the Food Channel, the Sports Channel, the Poker Channel, the History Channel, the Discovery Channel, etc. We are able to tune in these channels to obtain information that we have an interest in. The most important channel in our lives can now be put into operation in our communities. The new channel that is needed and can now be implemented will be called the **"Local Issues Channel."**

One of the main purposes of this channel will be used to implement ideas in our communities to lower our cost of living, thus allowing us to enjoy our lives, our families, our friends, the planet and our future without the need for making more and more money every year, just to keep up.

HOW MANY TIMES HAVE YOU HEARD THIS?

"I AM RUNNING FOR CONGRESS. UNLIKE MY INCUMBENT OPPONENT WHO HAS NOT LISTENED TO HIS CONSTITUENTS, WHEN ELECTED, I WILL LISTEN TO THE AMERICAN PEOPLE AND REPRESENT THEM BY CARRYING THEIR VOICES TO WASHINGTON."

OH REALLY?

A CONVERSATION WITH OUR CONGRESSMAN...

For the last 20 years, I have focused on the decisions that have been made by Federal, State and Local politicians and how they affected our community. The decisions that they make, roll downhill.

We knew that the loss of jobs, caused by N.A.F.T.A., would have a profound effect on our community, just as it has on America as a whole. When the economy really started heading south, there was another factor that facilitated its downward spiral. President Obama called it "real estate cancer." He was absolutely right.

Two other activists in the community and I decided to get in touch with our Congressman, Joe Donnelly. We believed doing that with what we had noticed happening in our community over the years, would be of benefit to the President and America. With Joe Donnelly being a Democrat, and President Obama being a Democrat, we believed that we were just two people away from, possibly, helping with America's economic problems.

The three of us decided to get in touch with our Congressman to present our findings and our opinion as to how to rectify the "real estate cancer' problem that was causing, at least, one part of America's economic woes.

The other two people that would accompany me were George Lane and Tom Zmyslo.

George had been a council member in southern Indiana for 18 years. He had been a participant at the Nuremberg Trials after World War II. He had also started the "National Flag Celebration." Tom was president of our township association. I had won the Dr. Martin Luther King Jr. Award in our community for my work on a plan to use communication technology to "give all people a voice."

George had called the Congressman`s local office, located in downtown South Bend, Indiana. He was able to obtain a meeting with Joe on St. Patrick`s Day, 2009.

The three of us met with Joe and his assistant at his office. The three of us were upbeat. We felt as though by meeting with Joe, one of the 535 most powerful people in America, we could really make a difference to help in turning around the direction in which America was heading.

I made my presentation to Joe. He sat there listening and saying very little.

I proceeded to tell him that we believed that President Obama was absolutely correct in identifying America`s economic problem as "real estate cancer." I told him that I had learned a lot about cancer myself, as I had dealt with it over the last couple years. I explained that I had prostate cancer. That prostate cancer was a cancer that was allowed to grow off of the hormones in the body. I explained that if prostate cancer ever becomes systemic, which means that it has gotten out of the prostate and into other parts of the body such as the bones and the brain, the final solution to dealing with that cancer is to castrate the patient, thus cutting off the cancer's nutrients.

I explained to him that, when a person gets cancer, they have three questions. The first is: Where did it start? What is causing it to grow? How do I get rid of it?

I explained to him that, if you look at the real estate cell, you will find that it is made up of three parts. They are interest, principal and property taxes.

I explained that the President and his advisors in Washington D.C. can throw as much money at this problem that they want, but it is not going to stop the cancer from growing.

I explained that the cancer did not start in Washington D.C. The cancer started in state capitals with the passing of "property tax." That is where and when the real estate cancer started and was nourished to grow.

I explained that when the Federal Government cut back on funding to the state government and the state government cut back on funding to the local government, the State and the local got together and solved the loss of income by realizing that they could raise property taxes to increase their tax revenues. It was like feeding hormones to the cancer.

I explained that the people in state government and local government were not smart enough to realize that every time they raise the property taxes, the value of property was being pushed down. It was like pushing on a blister. They kept raising property taxes, and the blister finally popped.

Not only was the real estate cancer growing, but it was also becoming "systemic." It had gotten out of the real estate industry and was now in the financial industry and the auto industry. This cancer had an effect on every industry in America.

I explained that now that the cancer had become "systemic," the only alternative left was to castrate the patient. In this case, it meant that state governments had to totally eliminate property taxes. No matter what Washington did, they did not have the power to stop it. It had to be stopped in state governments.

I also explained that property taxes were not Constitutional anyway. According to the Constitution, the only people who were supposed to have a voice were property owners. When they passed property taxes, they took the right from the people in America to own property. You can pay off your house, but you will never own the property that your house sits on.

I went on to explain that if we could get this information to President Obama and he could explain this to the American people and the people could put pressure on their state legislatures to eliminate property taxes, everything that Obama says, in regard to creating jobs and getting the economy back on track, would begin to take place immediately.

I explained that the most solid investment throughout time has been real estate. The economics of it is basic. It is simply supply and demand. There is only so much real estate and as the population increases, the demand for real estate increases, thus pushing the value up.

The problem is that nobody wants to buy something with

cancer attached to it. Cancer is a very expensive liability. An employer does not want to include someone with cancer on his health insurance policy. He does not know how outrageous his medical bills will be. The same holds true with property that has a financial unknown attached to it.

I explained that if Obama can address the real estate cancer problem by getting rid of property taxes, everything that he is trying to accomplish as far as producing jobs in America, can begin to happen immediately.

Once real estate no longer has cancer (property taxes) attached to it, the value of real estate will stop dropping immediately. People with money will begin to buy these properties up. They will buy them to live in. They will buy them to rent out. They will buy them to resell.

When they start repurchasing these properties, millions of people across America will go back to work immediately. When these properties are bought, they will have to be fixed up. Purchasers of these properties will begin to hire the backbone of America to work on these properties. They will be hiring electricians, plumbers, carpenters, concrete workers, bricklayers and the list goes on.

I also explained that with property tax revenues no longer being collected by the state and local government, that instead of sending our sales tax to state governments, it would be more energy efficient to keep our sales tax right in our own communities to deal with the issues that "we the people" think are important.

My presentation was over. I had presented this same concept to at least twenty people to get their take on what I would be presenting to our Congressman. I just wanted to make sure that what I was going to present to him made sense, and that it was easy to understand. Everyone that I presented this to said that it made all the sense in the world. Several people said that a third grader should be able to understand it.

The three of us waited nervously and patiently for our Congressman, one of the 535 most powerful people in America, to give us his take on what I had just proposed.

All that he said in response to my presentation was, "I will get back with you. I have to get to a parade."

The three of us were shocked. We all left and had the same impression regarding his response. We all felt as though we were talking to a recent lottery winner and we were asking him how he felt about the present economy. After all, in his life, what could possibly be wrong with the economy? He is presently making over $200,000 a year in salary and benefits. He has a guaranteed income for the rest of his life. He has healthcare for the rest of his life. Why in the world should he be so concerned about the economy? It is just fine, **for him.**

To this day our economy continues to get worse. In regard to our meeting with the person that we pay to represent us, none of us have heard one word from our Congressman. Once again, Federal Government is where good, maybe even great, ideas go to die.

THIS IS A RADIO PROGRAM THAT I DID IN EARLY 2010, THAT TALKS ABOUT THE MESSAGE..

Introduction: Now, ladies and gentlemen the nation's foremost roving reporter, revealing what happens when the world of the ruling class and the common man collide. Taking you across the Nation to offend the foes of liberty, seek real heroes and tear down the obstacles to restoring freedom. Here is "When the Worlds Collide" with your host Mark Anderson.

Mark: Ok, we are back on the air and we are going to get back with our guest, David Frank with "One Voice Now" of northern Indiana and he's got some very interesting and I guess you would say some unorthodox ideas in many realms according to many people's views of what I have been covering over the last twenty five years as a reporter, unorthodox ideas in terms of assessing and changing and reforming the system. A lot of it has to do with communication technology and my little rant before the top of the hour was about the airwaves and how they are monopolized by the major communications networks and their affiliates in one community after another. That is something that I have assisted Dave with a little bit, investigating although not as much as I'd like. I think there is going to be more investigation as to exactly how the network affiliates and the networks themselves control the airwaves especially in the age of digital television when the airwaves are carved up into lots, multiple channels, many, many individual channels that could be made available for the people. Uh, Dave, we are in a short segment now, but we are going to get into a long one This is a problem is it not, there is so much communication potential out there that denies the people to raise the issues and then move forward.

David: Yes, the people that presently control it or monopolize it, they really, I don't know, it is sort of mind boggling to me to tell you the truth. I have presented this idea to several broadcasting people, people who have the ability to change the format of their existing stations. Their goal is to make sure things stay basically the way they are. So the problem is that we are never going to fix America from the top-down. We've got to do it from the bottom-up. And when you look at what the local broadcasting stations are really pushing, nobody is really pushing local issues. I mean that these are issues that need to be talked about, the people in the community need to be educated on, and we need new fresh ideas as far as dealing with these problems. I don't know, it is like they would rather give you anything other than solutions to the problems. I don't know, you know they will play something like Rush Limbaugh which is fine and good if you like Rush Limbaugh, but all he talks about is national issues and what we've got to do as a community is, we can't sit around and wait for Washington, D. C., to come into our community and fix it or state capitals. What we need is to fix our problems in our community starting with the people in the community. We are all part of the problem but we are all part of the solution. It is just like your brain. If those brain cells are not interconnected that brain cannot work and the same thing holds true for the people in our community. If we are not interconnected, and we can now be interconnected with the communication technology that now exists, where we the people can start coming up with maybe a better tax system than we have.

You know, the Republic Broadcasting System, I love the name of that. My only thing is let's just bring the Republic into the 21st Century.

Mark: Interesting. What would you say to people who would say that the internet represents that new form of communication and that if the TV stations won't share their air space, let's just use the internet more? Does the internet constitute that system or is that only a part and parcel of something that needs to be broader and more all-encompassing?

Commercial :

Mark: And we are back on the air. We are talking with our guest David Frank of "One Voice Now." It used to be "We The People" in the greater South Bend, Indiana, area. What Dave is talking about is local in its application but the implications of it are State and National ultimately. The basic idea of course is to utilize existing communication technology and allow the people at a much more democratic fashion to raise issues and to bring those issues to the floor that our standard elected officials often ignore or downplay or water-down, to make sure that issues that really matter or different views on existing issues are brought forth, so there is a full comprehensive view of the problems and the potential solutions. From there he has a proposed electronic kind of polling, slash voting system that is different than the electronic voting that we have now with touch screen voting machines where we elect individual officials, or we make decisions on ballot issues or something like that. This is something different because it involves debating issues and bringing issues up, not simply voting on them. So, Dave, take it from there, starting with the communications part. You have all these things that get ignored, either entire issues or different arguments on existing issues that are never really heard, exactly how would this work? We are into a longer segment, so let's say that you are this frustrated citizen in county "x" in the United States of America and you see

48

something being ignored or some injustice happening. How would this work?

David: Under the old system, if you have an idea that you think can make the community better or you see something that you are not happy with, your only alternative is to go to one of your local politicians and plead your case and if he agrees with you, it may go forward. But I think that we are all starting to learn that Federal, State and Local Government is where great ideas go to die. What we need is a system set up in our communities where great ideas go to thrive. There are some wonderful ideas out there in each community that are waiting to be test marketed and so what we are saying is this, everybody has access to a television and everybody has access to a touch tone phone. What we want to do is use that television for something other than programming us to be oversexed and overviolent. We want to use that as a tool so that we can start raising local issues, letting people in the community present their ideas to make your community better, whether it be in education, environment, taxation, whatever it is. One of the issues that I think that you would be excited about Mark is whether the I.R.S. should have jurisdiction in our community. That to me is an issue that should have been discussed a long time ago. But anyway, that is an issue that we can present to the community over the television. We can debate that idea and video tape that debate, present that video taped debate to the community over the television, we can assign an issue number to it, people can pick up any touch tone phone, after we have built the community computer that contains your C.P.I.D. (citizen participation identification number) and people after they are registered to vote, can pick up any touch tone phone, call a local number, the computer will verify who you are, by asking you for your identification number and pin number, it will ask you what issue number you want to vote on, press "1" for "yes" or "2" for "no," count your vote, block you out from voting more than once. Every time that debate is replayed there will be an updated tally of the number of yes`s and no`s, so that at the end of replaying that debate over a period of 10 days, not only will the community be educated on the issue but the outcome will come from them. That information will be given to our local representatives so that they can start to make educated decisions as to what we want them to do. The problem in America today is that they do not want your input.

Mark: It's interesting because at a bare minimum, I am not praising or condemning it. I am looking at it as objectively as I can. I have some questions, but what it does do is it bridges that gap where the current media creates a chasm the people and their elected officials where once the people elect those officials there is really no longer any meaningful linkage between the two and the fact that the existing media creates this gap or this disconnect because they don't publish the elected officials voting records in any substantive way. There is really no way of knowing after you send Joe Q. Public to represent you at the county, state or national level on a concrete, tangible, ongoing basis exactly what that elected official is doing, so this amplifies the people's voice above and beyond the standard elections which are intermittent, here today gone tomorrow events and it gives the people a constant amplified focussed voice during, in between elections and in fact all the time. That is where the regular media, as you say, will show silly, ridiculous dramas like Desperate Housewives and constant sports and constant diversions. It reminds me of the movie "V" for "Vendetta" about that character "V," the revolutionary where British T.V. is all about diversions and cream puff news and cream puff TV shows and you have this ongoing trivialization where citizenship is trivialized, it's demoralized, it's watered down. You are supposed to just vote for somebody and just drop it. You are not supposed to say anything more. When you go to the meeting of the elected bodies, they often times do not want to hear what you have to say, and so you are left with this voting and do-nothing-else kind of situation. So, what I see here again is where the people could maybe acquire some of these unused channels in our airwaves, of all these different things that TV affiliates hold under their licenses, release some of that to the public, kind of a new public access plan for television and as you describe, proceed to fill in the blanks in between the elections and during elections because the media will not make that connection between citizen and the so called elected official. It just seems to bridge all of those gaps on a communication level of this whole thing.

Dave: Yes, you know, Mark, as soon as someone wins that election, the door knocking stops. And, the reality is, even though they call themselves "our representatives," they are not our representatives. I am an insurance agent. Whether I was an insurance agent, a stock broker, a doctor, an attorney, whatever it is, the only way that I can represent my client is to talk to him, to communicate with him. If these politicians, once they get into office aren't communicating with us, they are not representing us. So, the reality is that we really don't have any representation. Once these guys get elected they do whatever they want. Look, we have 535 adults in Washington, 150 in state capitals and 20 or so downtown. The question that we have to start asking ourselves is: if they are the adults, what are the rest of us? What are the 300 million of us? As you look at society today, and how society is no long maturing but actually immaturing, we are going in the wrong direction. What we need is a new system because if you have a dysfunctional system at the top, you will have a dysfunctional society all the way down. What we need is a system that functions for everyone and that means that we all have an equal voice. This is what this system can do. The postal service and the phone companies have already figured it out. What they did was to re-map America with zip codes and area codes. We now have the satellite and computer technology to basically re-map America. Think of America. You have Indiana that comes down as an elongated state, then you have Kentucky and blah, blah, blah. Think about how hodge-podge America is. The postal service and the phone company realized that they had to re-map so that they could get organized and get control over their business and that is what we have to do. We can now re-map America through computer technology so that it now looks like a honeycomb.

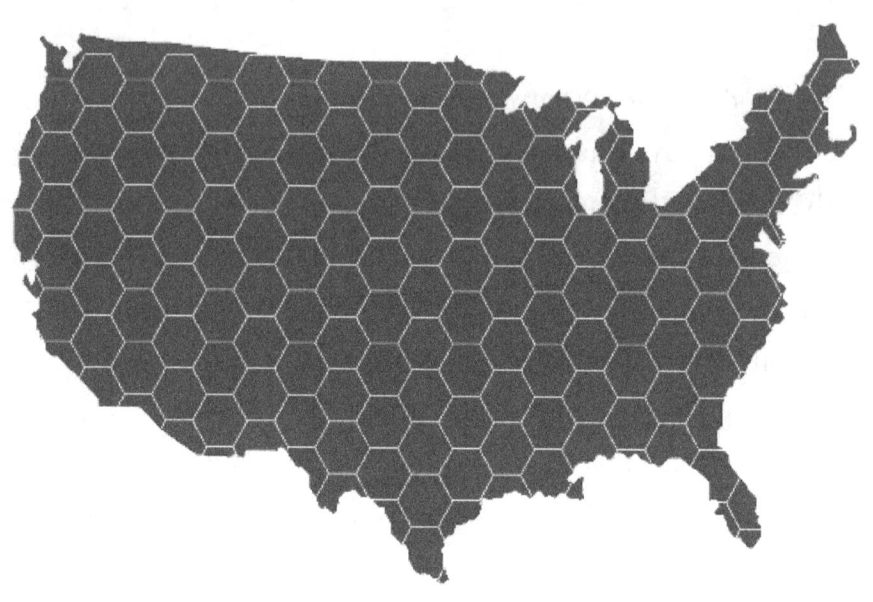

THERE WILL BE 1000 HEXAGONS ACROSS AMERICA

Your community will now look like a hexagon. What we are going to do is have the nucleus of that hexagon being a broadcasting station that sends ideas out to the community and a community computer that will have your identification number receiving the calls so that it is doing exactly what the human brain is doing. It is sending out information and receiving information. And what this is going to do is, instead of having 20 goofballs that are sitting on the city/county councils and a mayor doing all the thinking for hundreds of thousands of people in your community, what this is going to do is interconnect everybody so that we have hundreds of thousand of brain cells, (people) up and working. Instead of having seven goofballs on the school board that keep promoting a failing education system, what we might have is 25,000 people that start raising, debating and voting on ideas that start fixing the education system. We might have 25,000 people that start working on a new and fairer tax system. We might have 25,000 people that start working on the environmental issues. And all of a sudden across the country, if you just do this a thousand times, we can have nearly 300 million brain cells (people) up and working. Under the old system, this 225 year old system that was devised before the invention of paper clips and rubber bands, and if you had even mentioned the technology of the television, touch tone phone or computer they probably would have burned you at the stake. They lived in an entirely different world back then. The best guess estimate was that there were about 500,000 people in America back then. Today there are over 300 million people in America. That is 600 times the number of people in America and we are still using the old system.

Commercial.

Mark: Ok, we are coming back into our shorter segment with our guest, David Frank. We have been talking about his communication, slash, voting system I guess you'd call it. Dave, you just got done giving a pretty detailed overview as to what this is all about. There are a lot of bells and whistles and details that we could get into. One thing that I would ask in the short segment is that I talked in a previous interview with another guest about the problems with the electronic voting machines which we use now which of course are these detached machines that have shown to be rather vulnerable to corruptive software, hacking and different things like that. Do you believe that the system that you are devising or at least theorizing about could be made to be relatively free of hacking or manipulation?

Dave: I don't know if it is going to be absolutely perfect but it is a lot more perfect than the electronic machines that we are presently using. All that we are talking about doing is using the same computer hardware and software that the banks and the credit card companies are using to capture our money. We want to use that technology to capture the people's voices. When you call to check on your credit card or bank statement, they ask you for a group of numbers to verify who you are. It then lets you into the program where you can access your balance or change money around or whatever you want to do. All of the technology and software is here. I think that the way the people get frustrated is whenever they think about changing America, they always think about it by changing it from the top-down. It seems like too big of a job to even bother with. But the way that you've got to change America is the same way that you eat an elephant. You do it one piece at a time and you do it from the ground-up. You don't build anything from the top-down. There is a reason that they want us to believe that those 535 people in Washington can do that because what they have developed is a multilevel, marketing, pyramid scam. We are sending three trillion dollars a year to 535, basically lawyers, for them to spend for us, like they are our big brothers. People don't realize what they have developed. When you look at three trillion dollars, divided by 535 guys (for people who do not know), three trillion dollars is three million, million dollars.

It is the greatest prize ever known to mankind. It makes the Roman Empire look weak. This is an incredible multilevel, marketing, pyramid scam. The same thing is going on in state capitals and on a smaller level in your own communities. We can no longer afford to keep financing over-taxation and misappropriation of these moneys. The shortest distance between two points is a straight line. What we need to do is have a system where our money stays in our communities and it goes to places where we the people want them to go.

For 5 years I studied health care and I believe that "community health care" would probably be the best way to solve the health care problem, from the ground-up, as opposed to this thing that just passed in Washington, D.C., which is a top-down plan.

We need to have community health care in each community where the community owns the hospital, the doctors are on salary, not on commission like used car salesmen, and you educate the community over the television, radio, etc., on ways to take care of their health. These are the problems that can be solved but they are not going to be solved by 535 lawyers in Washington, D.C. We have to stop believing in Santa Claus, the Easter Bunny and the Wizard of Oz. We have to start believing in ourselves.

Commercial.

Mark: Ok, we are back on the air with David Frank of "One Voice Now." Dave, now that website of yours where people can check out the system; isn't that "onevoicenow.org"? This is the site ladies and gentlemen where you can go over what David Frank has been describing tonight. It is a lot to take in, in a way but it is an interesting and intriguing way of looking at things because the nation that we have is very, very dysfunctional and we have to sometimes think outside of the box to solve the problems and to move forward. We can`t just kind of languish in our problems and just sort of sit there in neutral. We know what some of the major problems are. We have private central banking that indebts the nation by the very creation of money. We have a monopolized media and not enough of the employee owned independent media in the print and broadcast realm so that the ideas and the debates that really should happen never really quite happen. There are too many diversions and too much false and misleading information. Too many people cut off from airing their opinions and ideas, and so by the time that you approach your government officials they can afford not to listen to you. The media is not going to bridge that gap or make that connection between the elector and the elected. And so we have some sort of dysfunctional and fragmented system where the basic pieces are there, but there is no real interconnection and no real listening going on. I don`t claim to have all of the answers but I have ideas on here that clash with one another. The job of a reporter really is to get the ideas out there and not stand in the way, and not only have ideas on that are totally in agreement of the reporter or the talk show host. Let the ideas flow and let the chips fall where they may. At any rate, Dave, I know that you have fought an uphill battle. I've kept in touch with you over the last few years. What has been the reaction to this system? I know that it hasn`t been a picnic for you but, how has it been going?

Dave: The local politicians have really fought us. They don`t want to lose control over the roughly 175 million dollars a year of our money that they are supposed to be spending in our benefit. They want to retain control over that money so that they can keep playing the games that they are playing so that they can keep benefiting themselves and their political cronies. Obviously, it is going on in every community around the country and every state capital. It's very obvious what is going on in Washington, D.C. I mean, let's look at it this way. These guys in Washington are taking (they can call it campaign financing all they want), but they are taking bribes from lobbyist representing special interest. And most of those lobbyists are lawyers bringing their special interest ideas forward and turning that into law. And so here we are; it is from the lawyers basically and it's of the lawyers, by the lawyers and for the lawyers. And to prove this point, not only are the lawyers making the laws, but when you turn on the TV, if you happen to be one of those people who are being harassed by the I.R.S., you are supposed to call a law firm. Or, if you are in debt up to your eyebrows because the people in Washington have allowed the credit card companies to engage in loan sharking, you call a law firm. The people that are on TV now are the people who are benefiting from the laws that have been made not to benefit "we the people," but to benefit the lawyers. And isn't it funny how close the word "lawyer" is to the word "liar?" Somebody had said to me "Do you know what side of an issue a lawyer will take?" The answer is: whatever side he is paid to take. And then the next part of that equation is "Do you know what a prostitute will do for money?" The answer is: anything that the prostitute is paid to do. So, the question is: Do we really want the direction of America decided by 535 lawyers in Washington or do we want the direction of America decided of the people, by the people and for the people? And if we want it of, by, and for the people, we need a plan. The plan is not going to come from Washington, it is not going to come from State Capitals and it is not going to come from the people downtown. It is going to come from the people. It just so happens that I am bringing this plan forward. It has nothing to do with me. It has everything to do with the American people. It is time the American people realize that they have no representation.

Mark: One thing that I hear in here and correct me if I am wrong, it sounds to me that you would be an advocate of the 10th amendment to the Constitution, at least in the general sense that you seem to believe that most issues should be decided by the States and the people, as the 10th Amendment says that any limited powers not delegated to the Federal Government would automatically revert to the state and local level, not just the States but the "people" as it says right in the 10th Amendment. It sounds to me like whatever you would have Washington do is extremely limited anyway and that the multiplicity of issues to deal with our day to day lives should be decided locally and, ergo, your system would be a means of doing that.

Dave: That is right. That is exactly what it says. You know, let the people decide what benefits they want from Washington D.C. Let the people decide what benefits they want locally. And, let the people decide how they are going to pay for them. I am an insurance agent. If I came over to your house and sat down with you and your family and said " Now listen, you are going to take these benefits and this is how you are going to pay for them," wouldn't you kick me out?

Mark: Uh, yeah!

Dave: Well why aren't we doing that? Because, that is exactly what they are doing. You know, all that the government really is is an insurance company. It is supposed to provide us with some kind of benefit. But what they are doing is shoving all of these benefits, that don't benefit us, down our throats. They only benefit them. I mean, they shoved Social Security down our throats and guess what Social Security is now. It is bankrupt. They shoved Medicare and Medicaid down our throats. All of these government programs that were supposed to benefit the people have not really benefited the people. All that they have done is take in our money so that the people cannot provide these benefits for themselves. What we need to do is give the people a "voice" and start really looking at whether the federal income tax was really ratified Constitutionally. Let's really decide if it is the kind of tax that we the people feel is fair and if it is not and there is a more fair tax out there, let's talk about it, let's debate it, let's vote on it and let's make it happen.

But asking the people on the receiving end of our tax moneys as to what kind of tax we should have is rather stupid, I think. If I could have a voice as to what kind of tax I think we should have in our community, I think it should be sales tax. The more you eat, the more you pay. It is very simple. But instead of sending our sales tax to state capitals, you keep your sales tax right in your own community to pay for the things that we the people want to pay for, and the nicer you keep your community, the more people will come, the more things they will buy, the more sales tax they will pay and the higher your standard of living as a community.

Mark: So what I am hearing here is, in a word,

decentralization.

David: Exactly.

Mark: Moving on, is there any risk in this system? We already touched on the question regarding the computer part of the system would have hack-able software and you seem to think that this is different than the software used for the electronic voting machines we have now.

We dealt with a little bit. Would there be any chance that the system in raising the issues and debating the issues would become bogged down in like bickering or bogged down in so many different opinions that it would lose a sense of direction or is that something that needs to be tried to see if that would occur? What you are talking about hasn`t really been tried so is that a cross-that-bridge when we come to it issue or is there a way around that so that things do not become overly contentious. I am just trying to cover all of the angles here.

David: We need a system that brings, in an organized manner, the ideas and the issues that we have. I can explain it very simply. It is really not complicated. After we have our community computer up and running and we get people registered to vote in the community, what is going to happen is that we do not want to listen to silly issues. We need a filtering system. What this computer is going to do is to pick 10 people every week at random. They are going to be there only one week for the same reason that the judicial system gets rid of a jury after every issue, so that the money and the corruption does not get to them. So now we have ten people that have never had an opportunity before to be a representative of their community. Dave Frank, average citizen, has an idea that he thinks can make our community a better place. He thinks that we should have a law that says "no driving and drinking, period." Dave Frank is going to present his idea to this ten member grand jury, if you will. If the majority of those 10 people think that this is an idea that should be considered by the community, Dave goes to the next step. The next step is video- taping Dave and his issue and presenting it to the community over the community television station for a period of 10 days at different times of the day. This idea will be given an issue number and when people hear this idea, if they have an interest in it, they can call one of two phone numbers that will be given. One number they can call and be part of a lobbying group for the issue and another number they can call to be part of a lobbying group against the issue. When they call either one of these numbers, information will be given as to when and where these two lobbying groups are going to come together and prepare for a debate. Thirty days later we are going to have a debate by these two lobbying groups and we are going to video tape this debate and replay this video tape over the television station for a period of ten days. Anybody that is interested in this issue can pick up any touch tone phone, (you can vote from an airplane if you'd like), and your call will go into the community computer. You will be asked for your I.D. number and PIN number, it will ask you what issue number you would like to vote on, it will ask you to press 1 for "yes" and 2 for "no," it will count your vote, block you out from voting more than once. Every day that information will be downloaded and every time there is a replay of the debate, there will be an updated tally of the yesses and nos. At the end of ten days, not only will the community be educated on the issue, but the outcome will come from them. We will test market that idea in our community and if it works for us, we will share that information with 999 other communities around the country and, hopefully, we can begin to start rebuilding America from the ground-up.

Mark: Ok, so you are saying that this filtering system and this ongoing debate and update of everything would have a tendency to mitigate against peripheral issues or trivial issues that could come up and to mitigate to a degree against any kind of over debate or overly contentious atmosphere. It would have a way of governing it in a way. Am I following you?

David: Exactly. It is basically one person raising the issue, which is checked by 10 people and double-checked by hundred of thousands of people in your community. Let the people decide if they want that as part of their community.

Mark: Now, a part of this, it seems to harmonize to a degree, with the 10th amendment to leave many of the issues to the localities. It seems to say that decentralization is the answer to leave Washington with a smidgen of duties and the rest would be done locally. It seems to completely create a new media system or communication system even separate from the voting or polling part of it. It just raises issues that would be far above and beyond your news, weather, sports your half hour snooze-cast would normally broadcast. It would deal constantly and consistently with substantive issues. No more canned news, weather, sports. The information part alone would seem to have a lot of value. The question then becomes to broadcast the idea so that people can learn what is being raised and debated and to hear the various reports. Along with that there can be local documentaries aired. I am seeing all sorts of ideas. Local news investigations that are not being originated by the networks. In other words, when debates and votes are not being shown, there could be lots of other worthy programming taking place. It would be a natural tool to reach out to the community for volunteer projects. What I like about it, although I have a lot of questions overall, it seems to give us an alternative news media.

David: It's a tool, Mark. It is a tool to bring solutions to the people in our community. If you watch the local news, like you were saying earlier, our local news goes from 5:00 until about 5 minutes after. They will cover a few, maybe, accidents or a fire or something like that, but none of the local media is being used to solve problems in our community. And that is what we need to do. We need to stop waiting for Washington. We know that they cannot solve problems. Look at the Gulf of Mexico fiasco. Look at what happened with the bankers and Wall Street. Look at what happened with 911. These people are not capable of solving any problems. They are only capable of taking money as bribes from special interests and lobbyist. They are laughing all the way to the bank. You know, we pay these guys almost $200,000 per year plus give them the best benefits in the world to represent us, but they are not representing us. They are taking the $200,000 but they are taking the special interest money from the lobbyist representing the special interest. Now, would you really want a lawyer to represent you like that? I wouldn't!

Mark: It is crazy and very frustrating. I do know that reforming the monetary system holds some promise because the debt based system puts everyone at the behest of the central banking cartel. I think that is one reason, a major reason why politicians behave the way that they do. They are under the control of privatized, centralized forces themselves. In other words, the bankers control the government and the government in turn controls us. But yet, there has to be some sort of system that redresses the grievance, in other words, turning that around, and I don't think that the conventional media system does not have the means of doing that which is why our broadcasting system is on the air. We need to amplify and expand that voice and that is something to think about. Summarizing comment when we come back.

COMMERCIAL:

Mark: Ok, we are getting into a summary of Dave Frank and "One Voice Now." Dave, this idea, I know that you want to get a prototype, I guess you would say, tested in perhaps your own community. I know that you would like to see it tried anywhere in America where it could take root and work out the bugs, whatever they might be. Do you see the current economic downturn and the distress that people are going through and the questions that they are beginning to ask, do you see better opportunities for progress today as opposed to, let's say, three years ago?

David: Oh yes. I think that people are ready. One thing that the media has done is expose the dysfunctionality of our present system. I think the people have reached a crossroads now, Mark. I think that they are at the boiling point and they are going to stand up with guns or they are going to stand up with their voices. It is my goal to see them stand up with their voices because we have seen what has happened in other countries when civil wars, or uncivil wars, which is what that should be called, break out. People are shooting each other and they do not know whom to shoot. It always ends up in mass chaos. And what they do when the shooting breaks out is they are fighting to see who they are going to replace the old goofballs that fill the political positions with a new set of goofballs. You know, we just really don`t need to do this any longer. The system has had its day. We are voting on American Idol. We are voting on CNN. We are voting on Miss America. Why are we not voting on laws that we think are fair and unfair? Why aren`t we voting on what kind of tax system that we do want? Let`s not ask the people on the receiving end. Let`s ask the people who are paying these taxes what kind of taxes that we think is fair. What kind of education system do we really want for our kids? Is there a better plan out there for healthcare that can be utilized so that people when people do have illnesses, they are no longer prevented from getting better because they are so worried about the financial burden that is attached to the illness? Or, should they just think

70

about getting better and not worry about the money and use the community as sort of an insurance company to take care of that benefit. These are the things that we can get busy on immediately.

Mark: I'm sorry, Dave, we only have a couple minutes left. Is any of this born from alternative political parties or alternative candidates that have been kept off the ballot by ballot access laws and other mitigating factors. In other words, is the current system not functioning because certain parts of it have never been allowed to come to fruition? Is it just because we have Democrats and Republicans that have a monopoly? If we got other parties and more democratization of what we currently have, do you think that, that would make enough difference?

David: **I think if people ran with this platform or put pressure on existing local elected officials, realizing that they don't have to run for President or Congress or state positions, but if they just either run locally with this platform or put the pressure on local politicians to build the communication system in each community, America will be back on the track to success and lead the rest of the world into a better place for all people.**

Mark: Thanks for being on the program, Dave.

Dave: My pleasure, Mark.

SO HERE IS THE PLAN: Rebuilding America from the Ground-up...

Either run for **"LOCAL OFFICE"** yourself, support someone to run for local office or put pressure on existing local office holders to use community tax monies, to "**fund a Local Issues Channel.** The 'Local Issues Channel" will be used as a communication tool to get information out to people in the community.

This channel will be used to provide three main purposes for the community.

The first purpose, is to allow people to present ideas to the community, that they feel will make the community better. These ideas will be considered as "laws" in the community.

An example would be: A law that says "no driving and drinking." These are laws that will have penalties attached. The penalties for breaking the laws will also come from the people in the community and be decided by the people in the community.

The second purpose would be to educate people in the community with information that is not intended to be a law.

Laws have penalties attached to them. These are ideas to merely educate the community, not punish them, on ways to make their lives better and better for everyone in the community.

An example would be: Educating people in the community about the harm that is done to children, either riding in a car or any other closed area, when they are exposed to cigarette smoke. The education of the people in the community can replace the thousands of laws and their punishments that society is now forced to live under.

The third purpose would be to use the station as a tool to promoter "volunteerism."

An example would be: I want to head a project to clean up a stretch of the St. Joe River this Saturday at 8:00 A.M. We need volunteers.

Without our 'Local Issue Channel" it would have taken about 95% of my energy to let people know about the project and find volunteers. By promoting it over our channel, it took only 5% of my energy to let the people in the community know about the project, leaving 95% of my energy to coordinate the efforts of the volunteers.

All of the three examples mentioned above will all be put through the first step of our new system. All ideas for benefiting our community will first be presented to our ten member rotating group of "Representatives" for their input and decision. Only the first purpose, ideas that are being considered as "laws," will have to go to the next step in our system. The next step is presenting an idea for a law to the entire community for their input.

The second purpose and the third, can be decided by the rotating group of Representatives, themselves.

Cost of the Local Issues Channel:

Keep in mind that we have spent over one trillion dollars promoting "Democracy' in other countries. The cost to bring our 225 year old Republic System into the 21st Century will cost a fraction of that. A trillion equates to 1000 billion. While promoting Democracy in other countries cost 1000 billion dollars, to build bring our present system into the 21st century, it will only cost America 2 billion dollars.

Once again think of America as having 1000 hexagons or communities. To transform each community, it should cost, approximately, 2 million dollars per community. This is tax money that has already been collected. This is tax money that, if not spent on a tool to give all people a voice in the community, would probably be spent on frivolous projects decided by a handful of people on local councils.

This money will be used to build the Community Computer containing our Citizen Participation Identification Numbers and also pay for the necessary "air time" needed on our Local Issues Channel.

Once this money is spent and the Communication Tools are in place, we can all get busy using our heads, our hearts and our minds in fixing our communities, thus fixing America.

I AM AN "ACTIVIST."

There are two types of activists, violent and nonviolent. I fall under the heading of a nonviolent activist, although some days I do feel like I'm being pushed over the edge like the violent activists.

Nonviolent activists realize that if they really want the world to change for the better, a world where we stop hurting and killing each other, the way to resolve the issue that you are concerned with is to promote its reality with nonviolence. It is difficult to do in this day and age especially when the people in power will do just about anything to hold onto their power. That fact, not only holds true at the top of the pyramid, Washington D.C., but at the state and local level as well.

It is no fun being an activist. I have lost alot of friends being an activist, friends that would rather talk about frivolous topics as opposed to "what is going on in the world that we live in."

When I first became an activist, people misunderstood the point that I was trying to make. They did not realize that I was concerned with only one issue. That issue was that we all deserved a "voice' and that going down to a voting booth once a year and voting for the "lesser of two evils" is not a "voice." They thought that I was a Communist. They thought that I did not love America. They thought that if I did not like our present system, I should move to another country. They thought that if I was not in lockstep with the leaders of America, I was unpatriotic.

They did not realize that I loved this country so much that I would be willing to do anything to save it. I saw it going in the wrong direction over twenty years ago. I realized that the only way to change the direction in which it was going was to take the power away from the few and share it with everyone and that Communication Technology is the miracle that we have been waiting for to empower us all. After all, it was only sixty five years ago when a few men in Germany showed us what a few people in power can do to ruin a, once beautiful, country.

People who you would think would support your position, whatever it may be, get to the point that they really don't want to hear about it anymore. They don't believe that it is possible for anyone to change the world that they live in, especially not you. They may support your position but they are not willing to give up their lives as you have. They may have an issue that is even more important to them, than yours is. They are just not willing to pursue it as you have.

There are literally millions of people in America and around the world who are nonviolent activists. The better known nonviolent activist throughout history include people like Moses,

Jesus, Gandhi, Martin Luther King Jr., almost all of the people who marched with Martin L. King Jr., Chavez, Jimmy Carter when he wanted the Jews and the Palestinians to shake hands, Mothers against Drunk Drivers and so many others around the world that try to bring peace and a better way of life for all people.

The nonviolent activist are a breed unto themselves. They are people who took John F. Kennedy literally when he said "Don`t ask what your country can do for you, ask what you can do for your country." They also took Robert Kennedy literally when he said "Some men see things as they are and ask why. Others dream things that never were and ask why not."

When a nonviolent activist has an idea in his/her head, they really cannot see a reason why their idea for making the world a better place should not come to fruition, that is until they try to push their issue through the political machine. Unless it benefits the politicians, it is easier to push a cabbage through a key hole.

The people that presently have a "voice" and have the capabilities of getting their issues passed into laws are the "special interests" that are represented by "lobbyists," lobbyists that are mainly made up of lawyers. Lobbyists write the laws and the politicians, pass their laws. Their voices are clearly heard because of the money that accompanies their request; their desire to have a law removed, changed or added, whatever action benefits their special interest.

Communication Technology and the new organization of America will now allow our "the people`s voices" to be the new special interests.

There are many people out there that could be considered as having a "special interest." Their interest though, is not about money. Their interest is an idea that they have to make America into that "special" place, once again.

AMERICA NOW FINDS ITSELF IN "JEOPARDY." IT IS IRONIC HOW THE GAME SHOW CALLED "JEOPARDY" AND AMERICA HAVE SOMETHING IN COMMON..

The game show "Jeopardy" was devised to boggle your mind. The concept is simple. The master of ceremonies will give you the answer. It is your job to figure out the question.

In America today, the masters of ceremony are the politicians in power. The have been giving us the answers. It is not only boggling our minds, but driving us absolutely crazy trying to figure out what the questions are to the answers that they give us.

Here are some examples:

The answer is ...In the 60's, it was imperative that America had to have a conflict with Viet Nam.

To this day the question still eludes us. The American people, some 40 years later, still argue over the question to that answer.

The answer is....America needs to invade Iraq.

To this day, we are still there and the American people argue over the real question as to why we went there in the first place. Was it Saddam's relationship to Al Queda, weapons of mass

80

destruction, bringing Democracy to Iraq, freeing the Iraqi people from a ruthless dictator, oil? Some people believe that they know the question, but others have different opinions. Does anyone really know the truth?

The answer is...Instead of having our children go to schools close to where they live, the must be bussed to schools across town.

I have also asked numerous people, including non-white people why it is imperative that we bus kids across town. Everyone that I talked to does not see the benefit of making kids ride on buses to go to school when they can walk to schools close to their homes.

The answer is....It needs to be against the law to smoke marijuana in your own home. If you do get caught, call a lawyer.

Most people that I talked to cannot seem to find a question to that answer. So many people who have run for President or Congress have laughed about the fact that they have smoked pot. One of the many who have admitted it said that he could not figure out how to inhale it, but I am sure the others were able to figure it out. If they admitted to smoking pot, an action for the rest of us that is considered illegal, an action that is considered a crime, an action that makes us criminals, why is it for those in Washington and filling other political positions when they admit to breaking the law, committing a crime which constitutes being a criminal, it is somehow funny? Is the question how do we prevent people from eating too many snacks? Is the question how do we prevent people from wanting to make love? Is the question how do we prevent people from driving too slow? Is the question how do we prevent people from talking about current events and evaluating the system in which we live? Is the question how can we fill our prisons with nonviolent people? Or is the question how can we provide the lawyers in America with more business?

The answer is: You need a lawyer.

It seems as though, alot of the answers that we are trying to find the questions to revolve around the answer above.

Answers to issues in our lives coming from the lawyers, answers of the lawyers, answers by the lawyers and answers for the lawyers all seem to be the same: "You need a lawyer."

It is all of the answers that all seems to end up with the same questions, that has jeopardized America and its people.

The answer is: Call a law firm if the collection agency, the I.R.S. for our present tax system is hounding you, your family or your business.

The question is; Why do we need to keep our present unfair, dysfunctional tax system? Why do we need a tax system in America that even the head of the I.R.S. does not understand and that turns us all into cheats when we try to keep the income that we earned over the year for ourselves?

The answer is: Call a law firm when you find yourself up to your eyebrows in debt because you are now a victim of "loan sharking."

The question is: Why would we need laws in America that would prevent the banks and the credit card companies from engaging in loan sharking? Why not allow them to charge 10%, 20%, 30% and more and allow them to add fees and charges that are outlined on disclosure statements that an eagle would not have the eyesight to read? When the Mafia was involved in loan sharking, it was considered a crime. The question is: Why did the government change its position on loan sharking?

The answer is: Call a law firm and they will sue anybody for just about anything.

The question is: Why would we want to live in a world where the laws that are passed benefit the law firms?

Hopefully, the people in America are now sick and tired of playing Americas version of "Jeopardy." It`s a system where the politicians, the lawyers and the special interests that pay them benefit, and "we the people" end up "Jeopardized."

OUR PRESENT SYSTEM IS NOT ONLY BROKE AND BROKEN, IT IS CORRUPT....

Today, as more and more of the media, are finally covering the actions of our elected officials, people are starting to figure out that the decisions that politicians make on our behalf are not necessarily just bad decisions, but corrupt decisions.

Is our present system in America a Democracy? Is it a Republic? Or has it evolved into something sinister? It is up to the American people to decide, but this is how I look at it.

Years ago, and still to this day, the Mafia used to bribe judges, police and **politicians.** They did that so that they could continue their business of controlling drugs, gambling and prostitution. It was also called "organized crime."

Let's take a look at one facet of their business. Let's look at the profession of "prostitution" and see if there are any similarities to our present decision making system in America.

There were three parts in the organized crime system of prostitution. Those three parts are the John, the Pimp and the Whore. The system looked like this...

Organized Crime's system of "Prostitution"

John

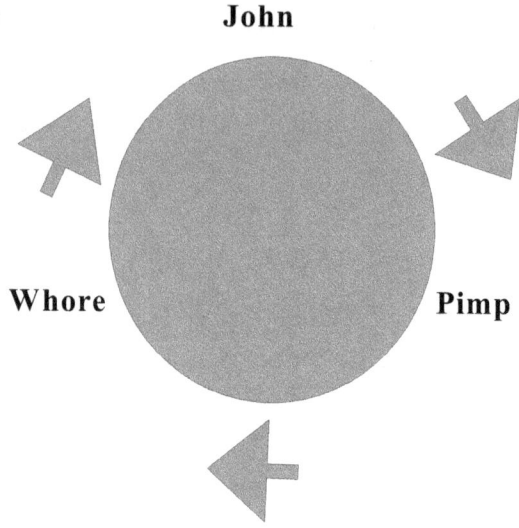

Whore

Pimp

This is a system of "taking." They all wanted something from each other. The "John" wanted something from the "Whore." The "Pimp" wanted something from the "John." And the "Whore" wanted something from the "Pimp."

It was called "organized crime" for a reason. If the John went out with the Whore and exchanged money, their rendezvous would be considered a crime. So they had to be organized in their dealings. That is where the "Pimp" came in. He was the money man. If the John paid the Pimp and the John and the Whore got together, no money exchanged hands between the John and the Whore: "no penalty, no foul." No crime was committed. In other words, they were organized in their dealings.

NOW, LET'S COMPARE THE MAFIA'S SYSTEM OF "PROSTITUTION" WITH AMERICA'S SYSTEM AND THE PEOPLE IN CHARGE OF MAKING DECISIONS FOR "US."

"Americas Decision Making System"

Special Interest

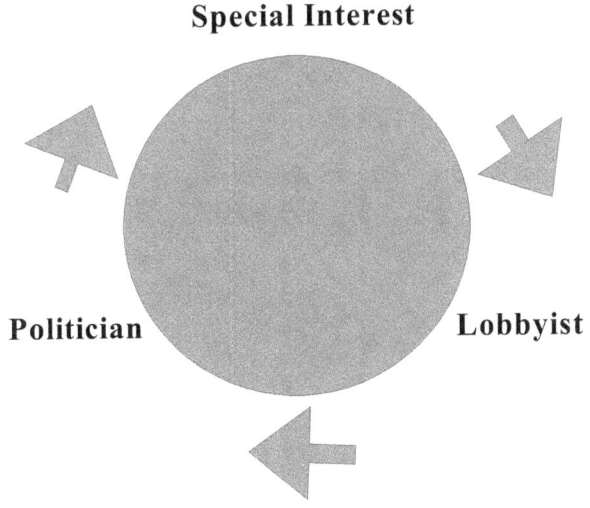

Politician   **Lobbyist**

DO YOU SEE ANY SIMILARITIES OR DIFFERENCES BETWEEN THIS SYSTEM AND THE "ORGANIZED CRIME" SYSTEM FOR "PROSTITUTION"?

They should both be considered systems of "taking." The Jewish religion and the Christian religion, on the other hand, the two religions that America was based on, were both religions about "giving." They were both religions based on giving, caring, sharing and love, the same concepts that most of the other recognized religions of the world are based on.

Our present governmental system has evolved into a system that should be considered diametrically the opposite of any of the respected religions of the world today. In fact, it is this corrupt system that is shown above that fills the government positions of just about every other country in the world today.

Ask yourself; how did the President of Russia become the wealthiest man in Russia? How about the President of Iraq, Iran, Lybia, and the rest of the Middle Eastern Countries, North and South Korea, China, the African counties and so many other countries around the world?

Ask yourself: How did just about every retiring Federal politician in America, retire with the financial status of "multimillionaire"? Ask yourself: Why is it when a Federal Politician either loses an election or retires, he becomes a "lobbyist"? Is it that they care so much about the welfare of the American people? **It is time for "you" to decide the answer to that question and many others.**

EXAMINING OUR PRESENT SYSTEM, LET'S ASSUME FOR A MINUTE THAT IT IS NOT CORRUPT. ARE THE PEOPLE IN POWER REALLY CAPABLE OF MAKING GOOD DECISIONS FOR THE AMERICAN PEOPLE?

My wife and I walked into a local restaurant one night for dinner. When I walked in, I heard someone call my name.

"Dave, come here for a minute. I have to ask you a question." It was Tom Pagna. Tom was a retired football coach from the University of Notre Dame.

"Dave," he asked. "What happens to a persons mind when they win an election?" Apparently Tom had just read an article in the paper that had upset him.

"Tom," I replied. "Let me explain it this way. Do you Have a toaster on your counter?" "Yes," he replied. "Tom, that toaster was built for 110 watts or volts of power. Do you know what happens to that toaster when you hook up 220 watts or volts to that toaster? Do you know what happens when you give that toaster too much power? The answer is it no longer functions. It becomes dysfunctional."

Tom smiled. "I never really looked at it that way before."

We are all wired for the same amount of power. When you

give any of us too much power, we no longer function the way that we are supposed to. We become dysfunctional people and we do a dysfunctional service for the people that we work for. It is very similar to the concept of "The Peter Principle."

Here is another example as to why the people, once elected to office, can no longer function. This example is on a local level.

Let's pretend for a moment that America and its communities have a system called "Democracy." If we were a democracy, this is how this issue would be resolved. The people would be able to watch the debate on this issue over their televisions and hear it over their radio. It could also be available on their computers via the internet. People could then use any touch tone phone as a voting device.

Let's say that 100,000 people decided to vote on this issue. All of the calls go into a computer housed downtown. The computer counts the "Yes" and the "No" votes and, because of ID numbers, blocks people from voting twice. Let's say that the outcome from this particular case was this: 100,000 people voted. 80,000 people voted "no," 20,000 people voted "yes." If we were a democracy, the answer would have been "no," and the issue would be settled by the people themselves. Under this example, 80,000 people would have been happy with the results and 20,000 people would have been unhappy. Remember, we are not a Democracy. We are a Republic or at least that is what our Founding Fathers intended us to be.

Instead of voting directly on the issue, on election day we vote for nine people to make this decision for us. Let's say that out of these nine people, five of them came from the column that voted for the College Football Hall of Fame and four came from the column against the Hall. By simple subtraction, there was a difference of one person that really made the decision to commit the community to this 18 million dollar project. It looks like this:

College Football Hall of Fame Issue

Yes	No	
20,000	80,000	= 100,000 total votes

9 Representatives

Yes	No	
5	4	= 9 total votes

In the above example, the Representatives voting for us, resulted in a difference of 1 person in favor of the Football Hall of Fame issue.

Under the example above, 20,000 people would have been happy about the outcome and 80,000 people would have been unhappy. This is an example as to why people around the world push to have the system in their respective countries be a "Democracy." In a Democracy, not only do the people in the minority and the majority always change, but a Democracy allows for the highest number of people to be happy with the outcome on the issues voted on. A Democracy makes everyone happy because of their "empowerment."

IN THE EXAMPLE ABOVE...

One person made the difference. But by going up to our system of democracy we had a difference of 60,000 people who said "no" to the issue as opposed to "yes."

The example that we are really seeing here is that in a Republic system, one person is given more power than 60,000 people. The Republic system not only gives the power to a very few, but it steals the power from many.

From this example, you can see why so many people in America feel powerless today. By representatives, issue after issue, experiencing this power, there is no secret as to why they change, why they become different people after the election than they were before the election.

The question that you must ask yourself is which system do you think is more fair for resolving issues. Which system do you want to live in?

Every person that I have ever shared this example with has answered that Democracy is the more fair of the two. Democracy is the system that empowers the people and allows them to intelligently decide and design, issue by issue, the kind of world that they want to live in.

IF THE SYSTEM OF DEMOCRACY IS A SYSTEM THAT IS OF, BY AND FOR THE PEOPLE AND FELT TO BE MORE FAIR TO THE PEOPLE, WHY DIDN'T OUR FOUNDING FATHER JUST BUILD SUCH A SYSTEM?

The answer is they couldn't have. They lived in an entirely different world than we live in today. Today we have technology that our Founding Fathers could not have even dreamt of. They did the very best job that they could have done for the American people with the technology that they had to work with.

They were inventors. They invented a system to take our voices to Federal, state and local levels of government. Two hundred and twenty five years later, the people who we pay to take our voices are not only not listening to us, not carrying our voices and, without a doubt, not representing us.

If our Founding Fathers were alive today, being the inventors that they were, there is no doubt whatsoever, that if they were given the assignment to build a system of government for the people of today, they would take advantage of the miraculous technology that is now available.

21st Century Communication Technology will now allow us to carry our own voices. We no longer have to pay these politicians to "misrepresent" us. We can now represent ourselves.

HOW DO WE KNOW THAT IT IS TIME TO TRANSFORM OUR OLD SYSTEM INTO SOMETHING NEWER?

Every component of our present system is faltering. The largest part of our system, as outlined by our United States Constitution, is the United States Congress.

The United States Congress is in charge of making our laws and spending our tax monies.

When polled by independent poll takers, the averages between all polls taken give the 535 people in the United States Congress, a 13% approval rating. These polls also tell us that the United States Congress has an 87% disapproval rating.

Once again, the United States Congress makes the laws that affect all United States citizens. They are also in charge of three trillion dollars a year of "the people's" money.

The 87% disapproval rating shows a clear majority of the people in the United States believe that these 535 people in Washington D. C. are doing a failing job. Congress has the most important job outlined in the Constitution. They are in charge of laws and money. If they are not doing their job properly, the entire government system is in failure mode.

We can continue to attempt to get this old vehicle up and running again. We can replace Democratic parts with Republican parts with Independent parts, or for less money, we can have a brand new vehicle.

America has always been the country to lead the rest of the world and has always been open to innovation. This new vehicle for America is the vehicle that we can all ride in together. No longer is there a need for a broken and corrupt vehicle that only holds 535 voices. Our new vehicle can hold 300 million voices. We can now have our voices heard cheaper, more clearly and guaranteed to get your voice to its destination in a fraction of a second, what other vehicle would you want to send your voice in? This new vehicle is totally energy efficient. 300 million voices can now reach their destination without having to start one automobile or pay for one plane ride.

Who better to decide the laws that you and your family are going to live with, than you? Who better to decide where your hard earned tax moneys should go than you? This country was not given to 535 people in Washington D.C. It was given to you.

YEARS AGO WE HAD A "REVOLUTION." A 'REVOLUTION" IS ALSO DEFINED AS "ONE COMPLETE TURN." WE HAD A REVOLUTION, AND WE ARE, NOW, RIGHT BACK WHERE WE STARTED.

People who lived back at the time of the Revolution were sick and tired of the King of England imposing taxes on the Americans, taxes that they knew were not going to benefit the American people. They did what they could to free themselves from their "taxation without representation." They decided to fight the British. That act was called a "Revolution."

The best guesstimate was that there were approximately 500 thousand citizens in America at the time of the Revolution. In other words, they believed that it was unfair for one person, the "King of England," to dictate to 500 thousand American people. So, they had a Revolution.

After 225 years and an American Revolution, the term Revolution has proved itself. America has had one complete turn and we are right back where we started.

Do the math. 225 years ago, one person dictated to 500 thousand. Today 535 people in Washington D.C., dictated to 300 million. That number equates to each of the 535 people in

Washington dictating to approximately 500 thousand people. Once again, the American people are sick and tired of over taxation, without representation.

We do not need to shed blood, for change, as they did over 225 years ago. Our Founding Fathers have left the door open for peaceful change. Instead of focusing our efforts for change at the top of the hierarchy, as they did at the beginning of our present system, change for the future has to be focused on the bottom of the system. By focusing on the "bottom" and taking advantage of the Communication Technology that America now has access to, it is now possible to bring about peaceful, change. The top of our present system will experience change through the use of technology and the power of 300 million voices overriding the 535 voices at the top.

Instead of a bloody Revolution, America can now experience a peaceful "Evolution," an "Evolution" that allows all people in America to have a 'voice' and allows all people in America to participate in deciding the direction of America, and allows all people in America the opportunity to evolve into "adulthood." We no longer need "big brother" in Washington deciding the destiny for the American people. It is time for "little brother" to stand up.

Violence begets violence and peace begets peace. The

Technology and the "choice" is now in the hands of the people. Technology is the miracle and the tool that gives the American people a "voice," that allows them to have a 'choice."

THE AMERICAN PEOPLE HAVE BEEN BEATING THEIR CHESTS FOR SO LONG, YELLING WE ARE NUMBER "1" THEY HAVE TAKEN THEIR EYES OFF THE BALL. THE BALL IS NOW ON THE GROUND. ARE THE AMERICAN PEOPLE GOING TO PICK THE BALL UP AND RUN WITH IT OR ARE THEY GOING TO LET THE POLITICIANS TAKE IT BACK AND WHIP THE PEOPLE`S ASS`S AGAIN?

Our ancestors came to this country to get away from greedy, hypocritical dictators. They saw, first hand, what the wrath of people in power can do to entire societies.

We saw a man in Germany rise to power, and we were able to historically see the metamorphosis that took place in this man and the men and women around him. The rise of Adolph Hitler was a near-term historical example of what happens to individuals when they are given the permission through their governmental system to make decisions for everyone. Absolute power corrupting, absolutely, can be seen on black and white films documenting the holocaust of an entire society resulting from people in "power."

When the president of the United States is Constitutionally given the power to wage war, every President that I remember, except for one, took advantage of the opportunity to drive

America's Military Industrial Complex. Some Presidents called these actions "wars" and some called them "conflicts."

Just about every one of these military skirmishes had the American people scratching their heads. America's leaders played the game of "Jeopardy" with the American people, where the answer is: "we need to go to war," the American people continually attempted to find the question that went with that answer. In the meantime, we voluntarily gave our sons and daughters to fight in situations that we never really understood. There was always one thing for sure regarding the wars that we fought. Military equipment had to be bought and when destroyed, had to be replaced. Huge commissions and profits for the weapons dealers and weapons manufacturers were made in the process.

The military is not the only place that we see "power" being played out. As most of us work for a salary, an hourly wage or a commission, there are no laws in place that prevent some people in America from paying themselves obscene incomes. To most people, these incomes do not seem fair and do not make sense. While we may work very hard for what we make, there are others who work the same or less than we do and make thousands of times what we do. How and why does this happen? Maybe it is time that we take a closer look at the system that allows this situation to occur?

We need to learn from so many examples around us that fair wages are usually earned. Obscene wages are usually stolen. If these politicians are making the economic laws that "we the people" live with, and if they are receiving money from certain groups of people, they will pass the laws that will benefit those certain groups of people. Referring to the special interests, lobbyists and politicians in the diagram shown here, the special interests will have the economic laws put in place that have been brought to the politicians by the lobbyist, to benefit the special interests.

LAWS GOVERNING OUR ECONOMIC SYSTEM

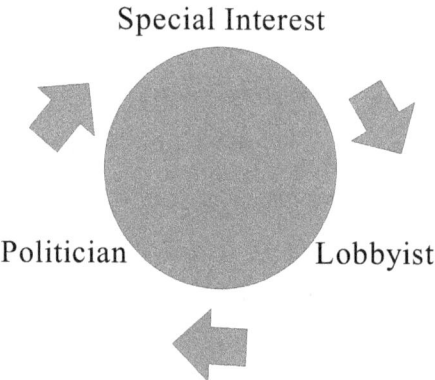

Special Interest

Politician   Lobbyist

The most important part being excluded from the equation is "we the people." How many times have you heard this: "It may not be right, but it`s legal." Our new world needs to have decisions made reflecting that what "we the people" believe is wrong is "illegal" and what "we the people" believe is right is "legal." The opposite of what our present system is imposing on us as a society.

Just as the weapons used in war can cause pain, misery and death for the people involved, too much money can also have have a negative effect on the people involved. Just as in war, money too, can cause people to go somewhat crazy. Greed is considered one of the "Seven Deadly Sins" for a reason. Greed is the desire for material wealth or gain, ignoring the realm of the spiritual. It is also called Avarice or Covetousness It may not have, exactly, the same effect that war does, but the desire to obtain money and the power that money creates can destroy lives as well. It ,too, can leave lives with catastrophic consequences.

The federal and state legislatures, make the "laws." These laws that are made at the top, decide what is fair and unfair in our economic system. As a result from the decisions made at the top, an extremely disproportionate amount of money is being received by a relatively few American citizens. Five% now owns 80% of the wealth in America. To find the reason for this is not difficult. If your country is not a true Democracy, it cannot have "Economic Democracy," a system where everyone is allowed to have input as to what is economically fair, as opposed to a few at the top deciding what is economically fair for everyone.

Without "Economic Democracy" the decisions that will make up the rules to our economy can be swayed, for the good or the bad, to affect different people. It allows the people at the top to decide who gets economic advantages and who gets taken advantage of. Rules can be made to allow a few, to take the money from the many.

The politicians take advantage of the system to not only benefit the "special interests," but also themselves. Take a look at your utility bills, your cell phone bills, your cable bills, your internet bills, gasoline, etc. They all have the Federal, State and local politicians taking a piece of all of us.

Rules have been made at the top that allowed a man by the name of "Madoff" to "Make-off" with the people`s moneys. To live a lavish lifestyle that most people could only dream of. It allowed the CEO`s and others at the top of "Enron" and Worldcom" to pack up the cash while the employees were forced to lose their retirement plans. All of these people mentioned here, and there are thousands of others, have supported the politicians and their actions, at the top. They have financially supported the politicians who make the laws, who decided what is fair and what is unfair. The questions that we the people now need to ask are: fair for who and unfair for who?

You cannot have "**Economic Democracy**" until you have "**Democracy**."

Democracy is: The "**People**" raise the issues.

The "**People**" debate the issues.

The "**People**" vote on the issues.

Note: When looking at cancer cells under a microscope, different cancer cells will have different shapes and structures. The diagram of the circle surrounded by the special interest, lobbyist and politician above shows the structure of the cancer cell that is killing America and its future. This cancer has become "systemic." It can now be found in Wall Street, America's financial institutions, board rooms in America's companies, State Governments, Local Governments, etc.

Just as radiation is used to kill cancer in the human body, Communication Technology can now be used to kill the type of cancer cell shown above. With the tool of Communication Technology and the power of "the people's voices," we can begin to put America's cancer in remission and get this great country up and running and feeling great about its future, once again.

I KNOW THAT WE COVERED THE PLAN ON THE RADIO PROGRAM, BUT I WANT TO GO OVER THIS ONE MORE TIME SO THAT YOU UNDERSTAND HOW ISSUES WILL BE PRESENTED TO THE COMMUNITY. THE FOLLOWING WAS TAKEN FROM OUR WEBSITE "WWW.ONEVOICENOW.ORG"

RAISING THE PEOPLE'S VOICE

When taxes are forced upon the public without elected officials asking the public for their input, isn't that TAXATION WITHOUT REPRESENTATION? The problem is that there has never been a way to ask everyone how they feel about taxes and other issues—until now. The area group, for "One Voice Now," has figured out a user-friendly way to make "asking the public" a tangible reality.

Here is the basic idea:

1) YOU THE PEOPLE raise the issues to make your community better.

2) YOU THE PEOPLE watch debates on those issues on TV.

3) YOU THE PEOPLE vote on those issues with any touch

tone phone

(The calls will be received by a computer to safeguard against one person voting twice).

Fixing America starts locally. The fix isn't in Washington, Indianapolis, Lansing, or any other state capital. The people in each locality, communicating and working together, provide the only way to build a bright future for our children and theirs.

Here's a more detailed description of how the issues will be raised, debated, and voted on. The process is as follows:

1) After the computer system is in place and people start receiving their voter I.D. number, the computer will pick ten people every week at random. The reason for this is we need a filtering system for our issues. We do not want to watch or debate issues that do not have merit. The ten people picked will be replaced every week for the same reason that the judicial system replaces a jury after every issue—to lower the chance of influence and bribery affecting the system. This will give people an opportunity they would never have had under the former arrangement.

2) When the people of the community have ideas that they

believe will make things better, they can present them to the ten members chosen through this random filtering system. If the majority of the ten believe that the idea in question should be considered by the community at large, the presenter goes to the next step.

3) The next step is videotaping the presenter and his/her issue, after which the issue is presented over an area TV station for a period of ten days. There will be two phone numbers shown on the video presentation. One number people can call and be part of a "lobbying group" for the issue and the other number they can call to lobby against the issue. When they call either one of those numbers, information will be given as to where and when these two lobbying groups will come together and prepare.

4) Thirty days later, there will be a debate by these two lobbying groups. The debate will be videotaped and replayed over the television station for ten more days. A new phone number will be provided on the video broadcast – a local number registered voters can call. Their calls will go into the computer.

5) When calling to vote, the computer will ask them to press "1" for English and 2 for Spanish. The next prompt will ask the voter to press "1" if they are registered and "2" if they are

not registered. Those pressing "2" will be informed on how to get registered. The next prompt will ask for their personal ID number and another fact to verify the voter's identity. Then the caller will be asked to enter the number of the issue they wish to vote on. Finally, the caller will press "1" for "yes" and "2" for "no." Their vote will be counted and they will be prevented from voting more than once.

6) Every time the debate is replayed, there will be an updated tally of the "yes" and "no" votes. At the end of the ten days, not only will the people in the community understand the issue in its entirety, but the outcome will come from the people.

7) To transform our existing system into a 21st Century System, resulting information will be given to our elected officials, presently in office, so they can make much more educated and informed decisions. Eventually, an issue will be raised in our communities asking the community if they want to continue to let 9 people on the council to continue to make decisions for everyone in the community or should we let the community make these decisions themselves. The results of that issue will allow a peaceful transformation from our old system to our new, to take place.

We could finally get busy fixing our communities and stop

waiting for politicians to try and do it with little in the way of broad, meaningful public input.

This is the communication tool we have been waiting for to bring our community into the 21st century. We can use our voice and our knowledge to reinvent our failing healthcare system, our failing educational system, our crumbling roads and our troubled penal, tax, judicial, and economic systems, etc.

THIS IS AN IMPORTANT PART OF OUR NEW SYSTEM. PLEASE TAKE THE TIME TO UNDERSTAND THIS PART.

There are people who are concerned that this new plan could infringe upon the right of others, such as people who are presently considered "minorities." Our new system has to deal with that problem as well. Please keep in mind that our present Constitution also has a part attached to it called "the Bill of Rights" that was intended to protect individuals and groups from being harassed or tyrannized by the Government.

Our new system also needs to contain that protection, so that our system is not used to step on the rights of individuals or

110

groups. Our new system`s **"Bill of Rights" prevents people from raising issues pertaining to a person or persons, race, religion, nationality or sexual preference.**

It would work like this: You can raise an issue to help poor children, but you cannot use this system to help poor Hispanic children.

You can raise the issue to build ovens in your community, but you cannot use the system to build ovens and burn Jews.

You can raise any issue that you want that you believe will be beneficial to the community; just do not include anyone`s race, religion, nationality or sexual preference.

EACH COMMUNITY WILL ALSO BE VOTING ON THE FOUR MAIN PEOPLE IN CHARGE OF MAKING SURE OUR NEW SYSTEM IS WORKING PROPERLY.

Unlike our old system where our citizens are asked to vote on candidates every year for people to make decisions for the entire community, the citizens will be in charge of the decision making themselves. In the past, they were asked to vote on the Mayor, City Council members, County Council members, Commissioners, Sheriff, etc.

Our new system will need only four positions voted for.

The first: The Chief Operating Officer.

His position: To make sure that our new system of decision making is operating properly; To oversee the workings of the new system and to identify and correct any conflicts of interest that may lead to corruption in our new system. The 'buck" stops with him.

The second: The Chief Executive Officer.

His position: To make sure that the decisions made by "the people" are executed properly. When a decision is made by the people, it will be his job to make sure that any law passed is entered properly into the "community bylaws." It will be his job to make sure that it is entered, without change, just like the community had intended. The "buck" stops with him.

The third: The Chief Financial Officer.

His position: To oversee the 'Community Financial Institution"; To make sure the projects that "the people" want funded are funded properly and without fraud; To continuously look for improprieties in incoming and outgoing flows of the "peoples money." The "buck" will definitely stop with him.

The forth: The Sheriff

His position: To oversee out "Penal System." Similar to our old system, he will have the highest position in the community. He will be the person, in charge of the arrest of people breaking the laws, not excluding, the three mentioned above.

THINK OF THIS NEW SYSTEM LIKE THE FIRST MODEL "T" BEING ROLLED OFF OF THE ASSEMBLY LINE.

With your input, this new vehicle will get better and better, just like the automobiles that we drive today. This new 21st Century system will be the vehicle that carries the people`s voices to their destination faster, more efficiently and more cost effectively than ever before. The **"T"** in our new model stands for **"Technology."**

OUR RIGHT TO HAVE A "VOICE" WAS THE VERY FIRST "RIGHT" THAT OUR FOUNDING FATHERS THOUGHT WE SHOULD HAVE;...COMMUNICATION TECHNOLOGY GIVES US THAT "VOICE."

The very first "right" that was included in the **ten Bill of Rights** was put there to protect us from our government. That right was **"Freedom of Speech."**

Our Founding Father believed in the importance of the American people having a "voice" so much that it was there number one mechanism for their defense. This new system now arms the American people with the "Freedom of Speech" or "Voice" that our Founding Father thought we should have, especially at a time like this.

WE NOW HAVE THE TECHNOLOGY TO FIX OUR ECONOMY AND MAKE OUR LIVES SIMPLER AND BETTER.

"We the people" are the generator that makes our economy work. We create the products and the services and we are the consumers of those products and services. By performing both of those functions, we move the money around the economy that greases the gears that allows our financial system to function.

Over the years, the politicians have slowly turned up the heat through taxation on a national, state and local level. The laws that are passed by politicians in Washington D.C., state capitals and city and county councils around America start out as "bills." They are called "bills" appropriately, and for a reason. Every time politicians turns a bill into a law, they agree to send the American people a monetary bill.

Here are just a few examples of the bills that have been turned into laws and imposed on the American workers and consumers.

Keep in mind, every time one of those laws is passed, the American people have to work harder to support themselves and their families.

> Sales Tax

> School Tax

> Liquor Tax

> Luxury Tax

> Excise Taxes

> Property Tax

> Cigarette Tax

> Medicare Tax

> Inventory Tax

> Real Estate Tax

> Well Permit Tax

> Fuel Permit Tax

> Inheritance Tax

> Road Usage Tax

> CDL license Tax

> Dog License Tax

> State Income Tax

> Food License Tax

> Vehicle Sales Tax

> Gross Receipts Tax

> Social Security Tax

>County option tax

>County wheel tax

> Service Charge Tax

> Fishing License Tax

> Federal Income Tax

> Building Permit Tax

> IRS Interest Charges

> Hunting License Tax

> Marriage License Tax

> Corporate Income Tax

> Personal Property Tax

> Workers Compensation Tax

> Water craft Registration Tax

> Telephone Usage Charge Tax

> Telephone Federal Excise Tax

> Telephone State and Local Tax

> IRS Penalties (tax on top of tax)

> State Unemployment Tax (SUTA)

> Federal Unemployment Tax (FUTA)

> Telephone Minimum Usage Surcharge Tax

> Telephone Federal Universal Service Fee Tax

> Gasoline Tax (currently 44.75 cents per gallon)

> Utility Taxes Vehicle License Registration Tax

> Telephone Federal, State and Local Surcharge Taxes

> Telephone Recurring and Nonrecurring Charges Tax

> Accounts Receivable Tax

> Recreational Vehicle Tax

We have become a society and a system where we work harder today than we had to just a few years ago to keep up with the demands that the political machine has imposed on us.

The generator or "we the people" have done a beautiful job at building a beautiful country. The problem is that the politicians,

118

with the decisions that they have made in our behalf have caused "we the people," the "generator," to overwork, heat up, burn up and freeze up. That is where the American people now find themselves. They can no longer keep up with the financial demands forced upon them by the political machine.

As the politicians on a federal, state and local level passed laws that basically stole our money, we have to realize that we cannot continue down the same path. As the definition of "insanity" implies, allowing this to happen to us over and over will not produce different results. It will only magnify the degree of our broken economy and society.

A person who fails to plan plans to fail. The same holds true with a country. America has never been about failure. It has been a leader of the free world and a place where people can come and experience success and have their dreams come true.

Top down systems benefit the people at the top. The plan that was given to me is a plan that allows all people to succeed, not just the people at the top. In the movie "Field of Dreams," Kevin Costner was able to reunite with his father many years after his father's death. His father asks Kevin, "Is this heaven?" Kevin replies, "This is Iowa." Kevin then asks his father, "Is there a heaven?" His father replies, "Oh, yes, heaven is a place where dreams come true.

America was once that place where dreams did come true, a place where visions become realities. Technology not only cures cancer, a condition that steals our dreams, our hopes and our future; it can cure the problems in America as well.

Even though not one person living today knew any of our Founding Fathers personally, we know that they all had two personality traits in common. Those two traits were intelligence and courage.

They showed their courage by standing up to the British and saying "enough is enough." They knew that by signing the Constitution that, if ever caught by the British, they would have been executed.

They used their combined intelligence to build a system that attempted to include as many people as possible in Americas decision making process. They did the best that they could with the amount of technology that they had access to.

Lacking today's communication technology 225 years ago, they were able to build three houses. The Legislative house that housed 535 people, the Judicial that housed 9 and the Executive that housed 1. If our Founding Fathers were here today, they would agree that those 545 people do not represent the wishes and the voices of the 300 million people in America.

If they were here today they would have three emotions regarding "changing our present system." Those three emotions would be "happy," "surprised" and "proud."

They would be happy and surprised that the system that they devised two and a quarter centuries ago lasted as long as it did. They never expected it to last this long.

Knowing that they decided to build a new system for America because of a four cent a pound tax on tea, if they saw the amount of tax that is being collected in America today, where those tax moneys are being spent, the relationship between the politicians, the lobbyists and the special interests, and the deals that are being cut on a Federal, State and local level, there is no doubt that they would be proud of the American people for having the courage to follow in their footsteps. If they were here today, they too would would consider our circumstances as "revolting."

They would encourage the American people of today to utilize the miraculous communication technology that is now available and build a better system for America. They would encourage the building of a better system that would include as many voices as possible.

Today`s technology allows all of our voices to be heard and allows us all to participate together in building the kind of world that we want.

TOGETHER

EVERYONE

ACHIEVES

MORE

IF THE AMERICAN PEOPLE WORK TOGETHER AS A "TEAM;" CAN WE REALLY ACHIEVE MORE? CAN WE REALLY FIND THE "TRUTH?"

I was having lunch with my accountant. He and I are great friends. He is a highly intelligent and is an extremely compassionate person. He had shared some concerns with me regarding the plan that I had been pushing, to give the people a "voice."

"Dave" he said. "I am just not sure that the "people" are smart enough to come up with the right answers to the issues. Let me tell you why I feel that way. The O.J. Simpson trial. Those people on the jury found him "not guilty." To me, he was as guilty as the day is long. If they were not able to come up with the right answer to that issue; how can we expect them to come up with the right answers to other issues?"

This was my reply. My accountants name is "Dave" also. "Dave, let me make two points regarding your concern. The first is this. The jurors in that trial were not jurors. Let me tell you why I say that. If you were asked to be on a jury, and the issue that you were hearing took you away from your family for over a year and took you away from your job for over a year, you would not consider yourself a juror. You would begin consider yourself a hostage or a prisoner. Those jurors had to be so sick and tired of hearing the lawyers on both sides of that issue ranting back and forth that by the time that trial was over, they had to be so sick of the judicial process that they were probably extremely exhausted and pissed off.

My second point is this. Millions of people across America and around the world, watched and listened to that trial for over a year. Do you think that, if the people in America were allowed to vote "guilty" or "not guilty" today, regarding his guilt or innocence; how do you think they would vote?"

Dave's reply was "I believe that if the people across America could vote on that issue today, unquestionably they would vote "guilty."

"Dave" I said. "That is exactly the point that I have been trying to make. Twelve jurors could not come up with the right answer. Twelve million could."

This is precisely why the politicians on a Federal, state and local level will not like this plan.

If the issue of a "bridge to nowhere" could have been presented to "the people" do you believe that the bridge would have ever been built? The same holds true for all of the "roads to nowhere" that have been built across America to feed the politicians and their cronies.

If the American people could have had a direct voice regarding the Viet Nam war, would that war have ever taken place? How about Iraq? How about our continuous stay in Afghanistan? How about the need to finance military bases around the world? The decisions on these and many other issues have brought America to the place that it is now in. It is no different than taking tests in school. The more right answers that you give, the more you "progress." The more wrong answers that you give, the more you "regress." Coincidentally, on a national level, it has been the answers that have been given by "Congress" that has caused the situation that America is now in.

The State Government and the local are not without blame either. They have each contributed to the unfair laws that we are forced to live with and the misappropriation of our hard earned tax dollars.

Going forward, it is important to remember that it literally took millions of people to build the roads and bridges that we ride on today. It took millions of people to build the airplanes that we fly in today. It took millions of people to win World War II. It took millions of people to put man on the moon and if we want to fix Americas problems that it is facing today, it will take millions of people as well.

America will not be fixed by one President, 535 people in Washington, 150 in State Capitals and 20 downtown. It is going to take the effort of millions of people across America. It is not going to be rebuilt from the top-down. It has to come from the ground-up.

The reason that politicians will hate this plan is simple. The political games are going to come to a stop. The rebuilding and betterment of America is going to start.

Our Founding Fathers began their new country with a "T Party." Their "T" stood for "the tea in the bay." Our "T Party" will stand for "Technology."

WE NOW HAVE TO REALIZE THAT THE COUNTRY THAT WE LIVE IN HAS THE WRONG TAX SYSTEM AND IS WIRED WRONG. THE TECHNOLOGY THAT WE NOW HAVE ACCESS TO CAN RECTIFY THIS PROBLEM AND TURN AMERICA INTO A MODEL FOR THE REST OF THE WORLD.

When a generator is wired wrong, it is only a matter of time before it overworks, overheats, burns up and freezes up. That is the situation that we now find ourselves in.

The shortest distance between two points is a straight line. Imagine a light bulb above your head. Why in wiring that light bulb, would you ever run an electric line from a generator to a point hundreds or thousands of miles away and then run it back to the light bulb? That wiring would be considered energy inefficient.

The same holds true for our tax system. If we want to use our tax moneys for things like healthcare, education, police protection, fire protection, road work, etc.; why would you believe that it would be more energy efficient to send your tax money to 535 people in Washington D.C., 150 people in State Capitals, so that they can send that money back to your community to fund the things that "we the people" care about? We have done that for almost 225 years in America and we have reached a point where the generator can no longer keep up and function.

The New American system has to rewire itself and understand that if we want to rebuild America in our own communities, we can no longer afford to send our energy (tax money) hundreds or thousands of miles away and expect that same amount of money to come back to us.

Imagine, once again, America looking like a hexagon. The technology is not only in place to give us all a voice in redesigning our communities, but the technology is also in place that allows our tax money to remain right in our own communities.

We have to scrap an income tax system that requires hundreds of millions of people each year to report their incomes to 535 people in Washington and 150 people in state capitals. In fact, we should have had a system in place that required those 535 people and those 150 people to report the use of our money to us each year.

The income tax system has really never made any sense. Think of it. Most money that is required to be reported by "we the people" each year is not income anyway.

Here is an example of what I mean. If you and I agree that it is worth $10 per hour for me to mow your lawn and I mow your lawn for a total of two hours, that means that I gave you $20 worth of my labor and you gave me $20 in cash. The $20 that I received was not income. You gave me $20 of cash and I gave you $20 of labor. We both broke even on the deal. The only way that a person should consider that $20 as income is if they considered the $20 of labor that I performed as worthless.

In other words, the labor that slaves once performed in America was considered by the slave owners as worthless. Unless we are all slaves, the transactions that we pay each other for are not income but a barter for equal values.

The income tax system that has been imposed on us for years has considered the work that we do as worthless and any money that we earn as income. This deception has to stop. We need a new and more fair tax system.

Not only do we have no jobs left in our communities because of N.A.F.T.A., we have no money left in our communities because of the sales tax system that our state legislators have imposed on us. It was a diabolical nail in the coffin, decision that is destroying our communities.

The sales tax system that the state governments have set up in our states, makes it mathematically impossible for communities to survive, thus making it impossible for America to survive. The whole of America is made up of the sum of its parts. Those parts are the communities.

The federal income tax money is going down the drain, but the sales tax is draining us as well.

Mathematically, state sales tax looks like this. Lets say that these two people represent everyone in the community.

Let` say that $100 represents all of the money in the community.

Under our state`s sales tax system, everytime these two people buy something from each other, the state gets 7% off of each transaction.

One hundred dollars goes from one person to the other. With that transaction, the community loses $7. The state gets $7. The community is left with $93. The $93 again changes hands from one person to another. Six dollars and fifty one cents goes to the State and the community is left with $86.49. As each transaction happens in the community, the State collects more and the community is left with less. Mathematically, it is only a matter of time until the State ends up with most of the communities` moneys.

The state does send a portion of the taxes collected by the state back to the community, but as the transactions continue, the community over time will have less and less available for its citizens. That is the financials situation that communities around the country now find themselves in. They do not have enough money to fund the things that they feel are important.

When our new Communication System is in place, the question regarding whether the tax system that state capitals have imposed on the communities is fair can be raised, debated and voted on, of, by and for the people.

By keeping sales tax in their own communities, communities can begin to rebuild. The shortest distance between two points is a straight line money from the communities financing necessities in the communities.

For whatever reason, money received locally from speeding tickets and other vehicular laws that are broken are sent to State Capitals. The state also collects State Income Tax, Occupational Fees, a portion of Property Taxes, License Plate Tax, Revenues from Lotteries and Casinos, and other taxes.

Citizens in each community do not get up everyday and go to work to finance State capitals. They work to support themselves, their families and their respective communities. Tax revenues obtained in communities should stay in communities. Communities cannot afford a drain the size of the tax revenues presently being imposed. It is mathematically impossible for communities to survive under our old system.

SALES TAX IS A FAIR TAX BUT OUR TAX MONEYS NEED TO STAY IN OUR COMMUNITIES. SENDING IT TO STATE CAPITOLS OR WASHINGTON D.C. SO THEY CAN SEND IT BACK TO US IS ENERGY INEFFICIENT AND STUPID.

Sales tax is simple. The more you eat, the more you pay. Want a big expensive car? No problem, just pay the sales tax.

Another name for sales tax could be "transaction charge." The credit card companies have been charging a transaction charge since their inception. Technology is what credit card companies have used to charge merchants and credit card users a transaction charge.

We as a community can now do the same. It is now possible to set up Community Financial Institutions in each community to provide the cards and technology to allow us to trade with each other. A transaction charge can be put into the system to allow, for example, a 10% transaction charge on each transaction, similar to a sales tax, to electronically be transferred directly into our Community Financial Institution. This money can be used to provide the services that "we the people' want in our communities.

OUR COMMUNITIES ARE NOW FINANCIALLY UNDERWATER. THIS NEW SYSTEM CAN GET THEM ABOVE WATER ONCE AGAIN.

I saw this story on television. There was a large ship that had sunk, right next to a pier. They were trying to figure out how to get this ship out of the way.

A person had an idea. He thought that if you shot ping pong balls into the hull of this ship, with enough ping pong balls, eventually the ship would float and they could move the ship away from the pier.

They took a large tube and inserted it into the hull of the ship. They attached a blower and began blowing ping pong balls through the tube. After thousands or millions of ping pong balls, the ship rose from the bottom.

We can do the same in our communities. Every time there is a financial transaction in our community, each transaction charge will be like one of those ping pong balls. We will begin to raise our communities above water and begin to raise our standard of living. The nicer that we keep our communities, the more people will come. "If we build it, they will come." The more money we will have to finance the things that "we the people" care about, the higher our standard of living and the happier our lives will be. This could never be done without the technology that we now have.

Obviously we have to finance a Federal Government. But instead of hundreds of millions of people each year trying to figure out how much we made and trying to figure out what we did with that money over the course of the year, we can now send our Federal Government a small percentage of the money collected in each community each year.

Imagine 1000 hexagons (communities) making up America. Each community with the push of a button can transfer billions of dollars to the Federal Government to finance our Defense System. This system will replace the list of taxes that were mentioned earlier because we will expect less of our Federal Government and begin to take over those responsibilities ourselves in each community. Performing these jobs in our own communities will put millions of people to work across America, but this time instead of these jobs being in Washington, they will be done in our own communities.

THE ROLE OF THE STATE GOVERNMENT...

"We the people" the "Generator" of this great country, can no longer afford to finance three levels of inefficiency over taxation and misappropriation of our hard earned tax dollars.

As we enter the 21st Century, we begin to understand the importance of energy efficiency. Financing these three levels have caused the generator to not only burn up, but have caused the societal problems that America is facing today.

Now that our "New America" includes it remapping, we no longer have the need to finance State capitals. It is up to the people in the communities where State capitals are located to finance themselves.

Once again, people around the state sending their tax dollars to 150 people in the state legislature so that they can send them back is energy inefficient and stupid.

If you take a serious look at the decisions that have been made in State capitals, it is not hard to realize that they have been more of a liability to America than an asset.

We compared the Federal Government system with the workings of the Mafia. We can do the same with the State.

The Mafia used to control and make money off of cigarettes,

alcohol, gambling, prostitution and extortion. At one time, all of these things were considered illegal by the government. They were also considered to be immoral.

Today the State makes money off of the American Citizens by selling us cigarettes that kill us. The State makes money off of the sale of alcohol that kills us. They make money off of gambling, that causes bankruptcy, divorce, depression, crime and suicide. They extort us by kicking us out of our homes and businesses when we do not have the money to pay our property taxes. When it comes to prostitution, you can refer to the chart on the previous pages that compared the Federal Government to organized crime.

When comparing the things that the State does to the things that the Mafia or organized crime was involved in, you decide how important the State Government is to your community.

When it comes to interstate highways, with communities coordinating their efforts with the adjoining communities, the roads once handled by the State can now be handled by the communities themselves.

THE NEW ROLE OF THE FEDERAL
GOVERNMENT...

For over 225 years, we have been paying Federal Legislators, handsomely for their advice. When they ran for office, they did their best to convince the American people, that they never made mistakes and that they were as close to "perfect people" that you could find.

We have paid them for their advice and we are now awaking to the fact that their advice was not only tainted by their relationships to lobbyists and special interests, but it was just plain terrible. Just about every issue that you can think of that makes up the America that we know today, is in the toilet. A mistake is something that happens by accident. A crime is something that was done intentionally. These bad decisions were not mistakes.

Our Federal Government needs a new system to help find the answers to our issues. The majority of these decisions will now be made and test marketed in our own communities. The Federal Government can now be used to facilitate us in disseminating those ideas around the country. These are the ideas that can make our communities better, thus making America better.

When America started, they had what was called a "Constitutional Convention." This was a place where people with ideas gathered. Our Federal Government can now be more like our Founding Fathers envisioned. It can now be a place where people around the country gather to share ideas.

When each community has the necessary tools in place to start raising, debating and voting on issues, it is important to remember that those issues will come from the people in the community. These people will be the new "activists."

Our new Federal Government can now be a place where people who have come up with ideas to make their community better, can now share their ideas with other people who are interested in being active in their respective communities.

The Federal Government will no longer be a place for great ideas to go to die. It will now be a place where people congregate, to have their ideas "thrive."

Every two weeks, we can bring 1000 people from the 1000 communities across America, to Washington .D.C. These people can be our new representatives in Washington D.C. We can bring them together so that they can share ideas with others, so that when their stay is over in Washington, they can take those new ideas back to their communities.

Just as Las Vegas is continuously hosting conventions, so too can our new Federal Government, 1000 people gathering for two weeks, with another new set of 1000 activist following right behind them. All year long, two weeks after two weeks, we can give creative people across America the opportunity to bring their ideas together with like minded people and by them taking their new ideas home with them, we can begin the rebuilding of America from the ground-up, the direction that everything comes from that is beneficial in our lives. No longer are we subjected to a top- down system that has been used to benefit the people at the top.

The Federal Government's new role will also include keeping track of issues that have been passed in each of the 1000 communities. As issues are test marketed in the community and then passed from community to community, it will be the Federal Government's role to keep track of the various issues.

For example, as my issue regarding 'no driving and drinking," issue number 001, goes from community to community, as it passes in each community the Feds will keep track of it along with all the other issues moving across America.

When 501 of the 1000 communities across America, adopt issue number 001, we will have a national referendum allowing everyone in America to vote on issues number 001. If the majority in America votes in favor of issue number 001, issue number 001 will become a Federal Law encompassing all of America.

If 001 fails to receive the majority vote during the National Referendum, it will remain a law that is valid only in the communities in which it has passed.

It was spoke of thousands of years ago about **a day that would come, <u>when the last would be first and the first would be last.</u> Today is that day...**

A CLARIFICATION HAS TO BE MADE REGARDING THE REFERENCE TO "LAWYERS" IN THIS BOOK.

When referring to the term "lawyer" in this book, the lawyers that I am referring to are the ones that fill our political seats or have influence on people filling our political seats.. I am not attempting to paint all lawyers with a broad brush so if I am coming across that way, I apologize.

Lawyers in our world fill a very important need. It is when they take over the political positions that need to be filled in our present governmental system that something unethical begins to happen. The decisions that are made by these lawyers filling political positions, have an impact on all of us. It is of utmost importance that the decisions that these lawyers make are made as ethically as possible. That is not the situation in our present system.

Somewhere along our history, our present political system has allowed our representatives to receive financial support (campaign finance money) from people (lobbyist) who have a vested interest (special interests) in the outcome of issues being judged.

Any person going through law school understands one simple philosophy. That philosophy is, if a person that is in charge of

140

judging an issue, that person either being a judge on the bench in a court room or a politician judging issues that effect the "people," if that judge ever receives any financial reward in the judging of that issue from anyone having a vested interest in that issue, he will be receiving that reward to render the **wrong answer** to the issue.

The Mafia was known for either bribing or attempting to bribe judges. They were attempting to manipulate the decision on the issues that the the judge was ruling on. Those bribes were an attempt to get that judge to render the **wrong answer** to that particular issue.

Politicians, many of them being lawyers, and lobbyist, many of them being lawyers, have been involved for a long time now, paying and receiving financial rewards to each other. This means issue after issue, in America, has been decided not of, by and for the people, but by bribery. If it is our goal to live in a world of the "truth" this action, that most people would consider a crime, cannot continue.

Communication Technology can now give us the opportunity to take the responsibility of solving these issues that effect our lives, out to the hands of the politicians and put that responsibility directly into the hands of "the people."

WE HAVE BEEN GIVEN LAWS THAT WE CAN START WITH IN EACH COMMUNITY. THESE LAWS CAN, ONE AT A TIME, BE RAISED, DEBATED AND VOTED ON VERY QUICKLY TO GET OUR NEW COMMUNITIES UP AND RUNNING.

The following laws are not intended to promote organized religion. They are ten common sense laws that will allow us, as a society begin to work, to live and love together..

We do, however, have a choice. We can continue to struggle with the thousands of man's laws that have proven to take us in the wrong direction. Or we can begin with laws that are much more simple and definitely easier to understand.

Note: if you have a problem with the word "God," just add the letter "o" to it and call it "Good,"

ONE: "You shall have no other gods before Me."

(It is time to stop believing the politicians when they try to convince us that they are the "all knowing." I have never met an individual yet who knows it all.)

TWO: 'You shall not make for yourself a carved image--any likeness of anything that is in heaven above, or that is in the earth beneath, or that is in the water under the earth.'

(We do this in America, but it is ever worse in other countries. The statue being pulled down in Iraq is a perfect example. We have to stop making people into idols.)

THREE: 'You shall not take the name of the LORD your God in vain.'

(If someone says something spiteful against my children, they are saying something spiteful against me. If we, as a society, say something spiteful against our fellow man, we are saying something spiteful against our creator.)

FOUR: 'Remember the Sabbath day, to keep it holy.'

(America used to be shut down, one day a week. Families were closer. They came together like clockwork, at least one day per week. Environmentally, we can lower our CO_2 output level. While the government talks about lowering our CO_2 output by 2% by the year 2025, this law will allow us to lower our output by 15% tomorrow.)

FIVE: 'Honor your father and your mother.

(Parents are the only ones telling their children that they should respect and honor them. This law reminds children of that, everyday.)

SIX: 'You shall not murder.'

(Before we engage in war with other countries, we should first run our actions past this law. War is not only responsible for killing people in other countries, but also for the young people that we force to engage in such an action. This law will force us to question actions such as war and other actions that our society has been involved in.)

SEVEN: 'You shall not commit adultery.'

(We live in a society where this action is not considered "against the law." Consequently, the victims of this action, the spouse of the person that engaged in this action, many times takes retaliation of this action into his/her own hands. Many times that action causes him/her to end up in jail or prison or even dead. This law forces people considering adultery to think twice, especially when there are consequences attached to their actions.)

144

EIGHT: 'You shall not steal.'

(Maybe it is time to ask ourselves if 535 people in Washington, 150 people in State capitals or 9 on the city/county councils, when raising their hands to take money from everyone in the community, without asking, and spending that money on something, without asking, constitutes the action of "stealing"?)

NINE: 'You shall not bear false witness against your neighbor.'

(In campaign commercials, politicians are always accusing their adversaries of something. Even if what they are saying is "false," it is not a crime. The politicians are at the top of our present system. Their actions at the top filter all the way down, throughout our society. This is a law that makes lying about someone a crime.)

TEN: 'You shall not covet your neighbor's house; you shall not covet your neighbor's wife, nor his male servant, nor his female servant, nor his ox, nor his donkey, nor anything that is your neighbor's.'

(Although the language that is used in this law, could be better related to by people living many years ago, the meaning behind this law is still easily understood today.)

THE NUMBER ONE ISSUE IN EACH COMMUNITY THAT WE ARE ALL CONCERNED WITH AND CAN NO LONGER AFFORD CAN NOW BE PROVIDED BY "WE THE PEOPLE." THE ISSUE IS "HEALTHCARE."

Without your health, nothing else matter. That is why the healthcare issue is the most important issue in our lives and our communities. The healthcare system in America can be fixed but it needs to be fixed from the ground up, not the top down. Sending our healthcare dollars to Washington or health insurance companies so that they can pay our bills is, once again, energy inefficient.

Our communities can begin to function like insurance companies. Our communities can provide their citizens with whatever benefits they decide on. People buy benefits from insurance companies that they cannot provide for themselves. Remember, we only want our government to do for us, that which we can`t do for ourselves.

If you want to provide your wife with $100,000 that you do not have, an insurance company will pool your risk with thousands of other people. In the event of your death, $100,000 will be taken from the pool and given to your wife. That is how insurance companies work.

Insurance companies do two things. They collect premiums and pay claims. We can do the same things in our communities. Individually we cannot provide roads, schools, police, fire, etc., but as a community, we can pool our money just as an insurance company does and provide those benefits for people in the community.

The same holds true with health insurance. Part of the money collected through the transaction charge and received in our Community Financial Institutions can be used to pay for our community owned hospital. The money can also be used to pay fair salaries to doctors and nurses. We can no longer afford to pay commissions to doctors. As a community, we can find doctors who want a fair wage and who no longer want to worry about the business side of running their offices.

We can begin to educate our community via schools and the communication technology that is now available on health issues and provide information that the community can use to take better care of themselves.

Healthcare can now be transformed, beginning in our own communities. When a person has a health problem, the last thing that the patient should worry about is money.

Everyone in the community is paying the necessary premium needed and supporting our healthcare with every transaction.

When you sit down with your insurance agent, you work together to decide what benefits you want from the insurance company and you both decide together how you are going to pay for them. The same can now hold true for our communities.

With the use of technology and a system that works for everyone, we can begin to decide, as a community, what benefits we want and how we are going to pay for them.

OUR NEW SYSTEM ALLOWS ALL OF US TO BE INDIVIDUALS. WE NO LONGER HAVE TO JOIN A GROUP OR BE LABELED TO HAVE OUR VOICES HEARD, AND MOST IMPORTANTLY, COUNT...

Our new system will allow us to be individuals. We can now stop categorizing ourselves and others as Democrats, Republicans, Independents, Conservative, Liberal, Minorities, Legal or Illegal Aliens, Gay, Straight, Muslim, Jew, Christian, etc.

Our new system will allow us to be ourselves. When we vote on an issue, all that the computer will know is that we, as an individual, voted. It will not even keep track of how we voted. It will merely know that you voted on a certain issue, and you cannot vote again on that particular issue.

This new American system will allow the walls of separation between religions, races, nationalities, low, middle and higher incomes and other factors keeping us as a society apart. Those walls of separation can finally begin to fall.

It will also allow the walls of separation between Americans and people around the world to fall. When they too, start using this system, they too will no longer have to be victims of the idiotic decisions that have been made in their behalf by their goofy, psychotic leaders, these people who have affected our relationship with fellow human beings around the world.

UNTAPPED NATURAL RESOURCES

With our new system in place, it is now time to start tapping into our most valuable natural resources. Resources, up until now, have been virtually neglected for the benefit which they offer.

The resources that I am referring to are the children, the parents and the elderly. By utilizing these resources we can begin to build a better world today for the children of tomorrow. The children and the way that they are nurtured is the determining factor as to the kind of society we are going to leave on this planet. With the proper input from the parents and the society around them, our children can grow with the attitude that there is a bright future ahead.

For the parents, the caretakers of God's children, all that they ask is the freedom to be able to undertake the task that has been bestowed upon them. They ask for the time and the money to be good parents and teachers of the offspring that they have been blessed with.

For the elderly, the people who have seen a greater part of the picture show of life, the knowledge that what they have learned can no longer be wasted. With the vast amount of knowledge that they have collected over the many years of their lives, we can no longer allow them to rot in nursing and old folks homes like wasted pieces of garbage.

Just like everything else coming from our old dysfunctional system, it is all backwards. Instead of not using and wasting the knowledge that lies in the hearts and the minds of the elderly, with our new system we can now tap into information that is just waiting for us, like diamonds waiting to be uncovered.

By giving the children a world that they can look forward to living in, allowing the parents to complete their parental duties and no longer wasting the elderly and the knowledge that they have for all of us, our greatest natural resources can finally be put to use.

WE ARE ALL VESSELS

Just as the blood vessels within your body, bring your cells the life giving nutrients that they need, the same holds true for America and its people.

The American people are like the vessels within your body. The people, also, can bring life-giving nutrients to America. Vessels are used to funnel life-giving oxygen to the cells which make up your body. People are the channels, the vessels, that bring life-giving ideas to be shared with the rest of America and even the rest of the world.

When vessels are blocked in your body, the life-giving nutrients don't get to the rest of the cells and they begin to die. Up until now, the life-giving ideas that the people have to share with the rest of us have been blocked. That is why we are experiencing the symptoms of a dying country.

Modern doctors use new technological devices to unblock arteries so that the vessels are once again free to bring life-giving nutrients to the rest of the body. Through the technology mentioned in this book, we the people can free up those vessels that have been blocked, so that they can finally deliver their life saving ideas and nutrients to the rest of the country and world.

It is easy to see why people have been acting the way that they have. They are trying to survive within a system whose arteries are blocked and whose heart is dying.

Ask yourself: How would you live the rest of your life if you went to the doctor today and he told you that your heart was dying? How would you feel if he told you that the only chance you have for any kind of future, would be an entirely new heart, a heart strong enough to pump the nutrients that your entire body needs to survive.

Years ago the outcome would be terminal. Before modern technology, when a heart no longer functioned effectively, people went home and waited to die. Today we live in a new world, a world where the miracle of technology can now allow once terminal people to live a normal life.

Although many people think there is no hope for fixing America, just like modern-day doctors we can fix the heart and open the vessels so that they can, once again, deliver life-giving nutrients to the rest of us and the world.

These nutritional ideas that the people, our vessels, are waiting to deliver can now be enjoyed by all. As we use modern day Communication Technology to build a platform where these ideas can be heard and considered, America can look forward to a bright future just like a heart patient with a brand new heart. The ideas pertaining to Issues mentioned earlier are just ideas. They are no different than other ideas that are in the hearts and minds of millions of people. These ideas are just waiting to be heard.

The new system for America is more than just an idea. It was an idea that was implanted in me. It was an idea that I, as a vessel, am being used to bring to you.

Your self-empowerment is a necessity if you wish to leave your children a world that is one of freedom and liberty. This is the idea that was given to me, so that you can participate in the changing of America the changing of the guard, from the present owners, the politicians, to the rightful owners, the people themselves.

The blueprint is here for the taking. It is a blueprint that works. It is a blueprint for the building of a functional system leading to a functional society. It is a blueprint for the step by step takeover of a country that was given to you, the people.

Sit back and do nothing, or **participate by running for local office**. Listen to political rhetoric for the rest of your life, or listen to common sense ideas that you and your family can vote on . Vote for a politician every year or two or vote frequently on ideas that will change the world in which you live.

God has given every human being a superior mind. We are the "master link" on this planet. The decisions that we make today, will not only have an effect on every living creature on the planet, but the planet itself. This mind is to be used to take in information, process it and use it. Are we going to let our greatest God-given gift go to waste, or are we going to show our appreciation for it by using it on a daily basis?

WE HAVE TO LEARN HOW TO PRAY OR WE ARE GOING TO CONTINUE TO BE PREY.

The action of praying does not necessarily mean that it has to be done in a church or synagogue or mosque. The act of praying anywhere is simply our request to God to provide us with the right answers to the questions that we have in our lives.

One of the biggest problems that Americans have today is that they have never been taught how to pray. They have been led to believe by church leaders and politicians that if you give your questions to them, they will answer your questions for you. We have always looked toward another individual for the answers in our lives. Our new system puts the emphasis for decision making on the people themselves. It forces them to look inward, not outward, for the answers that they request.

By practicing the art of asking the person inside of us for the right answers, we will begin to look upon ourselves with a new respect that we've never felt before. We will begin to look upon ourselves with the envy that we once had for other people, the people in power, people who at one time convinced us that they had all of the right answers for everyone and the world in which we live.

Frustration has been felt by the majority of Americans as we work hard to earn our living and someone other than us ends up with the fruits of our labor. Those someones include. Utility companies, doctors and hospitals, lawyers, insurance companies, loan institutions, and the politicians in the form of our taxes.

We have felt for a long time that, just like the tiger and the deer, someone else is controlling our lives. Someone else is controlling our destinies.

A predator-prey relationship is the same scenario. A predator controls the destiny of its prey. Through the magic of our voices, we can begin to relieve ourselves of those Issues that have been holding us captive. We can now begin to feel free. We no longer have to feel like "prey."

A new system of praying will evolve from our society. A practice of looking for a spiritual answer that can now be found in each and every one of us. It can be realized like never before. The unleashing of this spirituality is the only way to go back to where we've been, to restart our journey in a new direction, a start down the right path, a path leading to our new world.

A world no longer of political promises. A world that promises everything that we are willing to sacrifice for. A world of fairness and love. A world of "doing unto others as we would have others do unto us." A world where the decisions that we personally make together are the decisions that will affect our lives as well as others. A world that allows our society to evolve into adulthood. It will be those decisions that will be the "truth" that shall make us "free."

THE "NEW WORLD"

A GOVERNMENT "BY THE PEOPLE"

We are like the first people getting ready to enter a brand new world. We are no different than the first person, tens of thousands of years ago, entering the world that we know of today.

As that first person began to explore his new world, he came upon a nut-bearing tree. After he picked up the nut, he looked at it, smelled it, squeezed it, bit it and probably jumped on it. He had a suspicion that there was something special inside of that nut that, if he could just get into it, he would enjoy.

Even for the very first person on the planet, it was only a matter of time before he figured out that if he ever wanted to enjoy the meat inside that nut, he would need something other than just himself to get to it. In order to enjoy what that nut had to offer, he would have to devise a tool. At that time, a simple rock sufficed as the tool that our oldest ancestor used to nourish his life with the fruit that the nut had to offer.

Countless years later, nothing has really changed. We instinctively feel that there is something waiting to provide us with the nourishment that we desire. We smell it. We feel it. We can even taste it. We truly believe, in a half frightened way, that there is a better world waiting for us, a world where not only our hunger will be quenched, but the hunger of everyone. We, just like our oldest ancestor, just were not sure how to get into it.

Even though we are more intelligent and we live in an entirely different world, we must go back and learn from him. We must learn that anything that we want in life, anything that we wish to build, takes exactly what it took many years ago. It takes a "tool" and a way to use that "tool."

Your "tool" and its instructions, the "system" and how to use it have been explained and outlined in this book. It is just the beginning of a "New World" that God wants for His children that He loves very much. All He asks is that we use it for our benefit and the benefit of others.

Ladies and gentlemen, technology is the miracle that we have been waiting for. It has been right in front of us all along. It was put here for our benefit. It is here for the taking.

God has answered our prayers for a better life. He wants to give us a better world, a world that we can enjoy. It is the same desire that we as parents have for our children, a better world that they can all enjoy, a world that must be taken care of by no one other than ourselves. This world of beauty and freedom can and will be built by us. That is why **He** has provided us with the necessary tools.

Your voice is the ticket to make sure that the freedom that we have requested stays with us forever. The technology and the system that I have presented you with is the Colliseum to bring us all together.

AMERICA IS JUST LIKE THE MOVIE "ROCKIE."

America now finds itself in the same situation as the character "Rockie." In his first movie, Rockie became overwhelmed with the problems in his life. His wife was experiencing a life and death situation.

And then, while his wife lay there in her bed, her eyes opened. His wife knew that Rockie was armed with the tools to win his fight. With one word from her, Rockie was able to pick himself up and fight the fight that he knew that he was capable of winning. That word was "**win**."

Just like Rockie, the American People are overwhelmed with the problems in their lives but, just like Rockie, they are now armed with the tools to **win** their fight.

Their fight is not in the ring. Their fight is across the country. Their fight is to rebuild the 'greatest country on earth" and in the process show people around the world how they can make their countries great as well.

God has given us the tools to win our fight. It is now up to us to pick those tools up and, just like Rockie making his wife proud, "we the people" can pick up the tools that God has given us and make Him proud.

THE VOICE THAT WE HAVE TOGETHER, IS THE VOICE TO TAKE US IN THE RIGHT DIRECTION. IT IS THE MOST SPECIAL VOICE IN THE WORLD.

Today, we find people lost and insecure. We find people looking in many directions for a new and better life. Several brilliant people who once visited our planet, left us with important clues to let us know that this plan is the right direction for our future.

Albert Einstein was able to understand the vast darkness of the universe by one simple statement. He said that "everything is relative." By realizing that, he was able to understand complicated things by relating them to relatively simple things. We, too, can begin to understand the magnitude of where we now find ourselves and where we can now go.

Thomas Edison possessed an idea that he just knew would change the entire world. He knew that he could turn darkness into light. He knew that if he could just find the right components and combine those components with the right system, he could harness enough energy to create light. The trick was bringing all that energy together in just one place. He soon created the light bulb. He changed our world completely.

The new system that we can now build is the same as Edison's light bulb. It can not only change our world, it can also light our way.

TECHNOLOGY IS THE MIRACLE THAT HAS BEEN GIVEN TO US SO THAT WE CAN BEGIN TO LEARN MORE ABOUT OURSELVES AND OUR FELLOW MAN...

Because of the technological tools that we now have access to, we have been able to learn quite a bit about ourselves. Through the study of genetics, we have learned that genetically, you have a piece of your father in you. Genetically you have a piece of your grandfather, your great grandfather, your great, great and so on. If we go back enough generations, we all have a piece of our Creator in us. That is probably why we are "creative people." That is probably why we have been chosen and given the tools to build a bright new world.

How do we build this "new world"? In today's money, that is the sixty four billion dollar question. Where do we get our direction? Who is going to tell us how?

Although we know that our new system of "Democracy" is a "Government of the People," how do we know that this is the tool that we need to take us in the right direction?

"Vox Populi, Vox Dei"

"The Voice of the People, is the Voice of God."

Our new system that we are about to build is just like Edison's light bulb. Just as Edison's bulb was the tool to bring watts and volts of electricity together to create light, so too does our new tool.

Our new tool and system brings "the people" together with ideas. Each and every one of us, having a piece of our creator inside of us, can now be used to bring watts and volts of our Creator, together. Just as Edison's bulb, something even more powerful than electricity can now be used to light our way.

My goal was to share this information with you. It was to get you to understand how we can build a new system that derives its information from a place called the "Know Zone." The "know zone" is right where the phrase implies. It is located right behind your nose. We know that it is the "Truth" that shall make us free and it is the "know zone" that will help us find that "truth."

I pray that all of this makes sense to you. I pray that it is something that you too believe in. I am going to continue to do my best to get this information out to as many people as possible. I cannot do it alone. But, with your help, we can not only move a mountain, we can also build a better world. We cannot walk away from this life and leave it up to our children to clean up. We the adults, coming together with the same idea, an idea that is simple and doable, can leave this great country in better shape than we found it. Together we can all make a difference.

Please remember, "Vox Populi, Vox Dei."

"The Voice of the People, is the Voice of God".

Please share this book with your family, friends and everyone who is concerned about the future of America and the world.

Thank you for your time...

www.ingramcontent.com/pod-product-compliance
Lightning Source LLC
Chambersburg PA
CBHW062207280526
45788CB00001B/484